Men's Guide to Bread Machine Baking

Men's Guide
to Bread
Machine Baking

Making Pizza, Bagels, Beer Bread, Pretzels,
Sourdough, and over 100 Other Great Breads
with Your Bread Machine

Jeffrey Gerlach

PRIMA PUBLISHING

PRIMA PUBLISHING and colophon are registered trademarks of Prima Communications, Inc.

Library of Congress Cataloging-in-Publication Data

Gerlach, Jeffrey.
   Men's guide to bread machine baking: making pizza, bagels, beer bread, pretzels, sourdough, and over 100 other great breads with your bread machine / Jeffrey Gerlach.
     p.   cm.
  Includes index.
  ISBN 0-7615-0652-7
  1. Bread.   2. Automatic bread machines.   I. Title.
TX769.G472   1996
641.8'15—dc20   96-29194
                                                 CIP

96 97 98 99 00 01 HH 10 9 8 7 6 5 4 3 2 1
Printed in the United States of America

How to Order
Single copies may be ordered from Prima Publishing, P.O. Box 1260BK, Rocklin, CA 95677; telephone (916) 632-4400. Quantity discounts are also available. On your letterhead, include information concerning the intended use of the books and the number of books you wish to purchase.

Visit us online at http://www.primapublishing.com

For Nancy
Thanks for putting up with all the madness!

CONTENTS

CHAPTER 4

Bread-Making Techniques   34

CHAPTER 5

Bread and Dough Miscellany   41

CHAPTER 6

Trouble-Shooting   48

CHAPTER 7

Other Helpful Tools   53

PART II: Bread Machine Recipes   55

CHAPTER 8

White, Egg, and Sourdough Loaves   57

CHAPTER 16

Soft Pretzels and Breadsticks   150

CHAPTER 17

Pizza and Focaccia   155

CHAPTER 18

Breakfast Breads   165

ACKNOWLEDGMENTS

I am indebted to the following people for all their unselfish help, which included, among other things, creating and donating recipes, testing recipes, answering innumerable questions, keeping a sense of humor while tasting endless loaves of bread, and dropping over at just the right time with a cold six pack. After all, man does not live by bread alone! Sincere thanks to: Francie and Mark Deter, Dave DeWitt, Robert Dillingham, John Gerlach, Mark Gerlach, Tim Huff, Robert Katz, Robert McDonald, Neil Mann, Leif Nielsen, Don Schwebach, Mike Touby, Joanne Turchany, Steve Vigil, and Paul Willis, and lastly, Jennifer Basye Sander for this opportunity!

INTRODUCTION

Life in the '90s has most of us stuck in the fast lane, and quality of life and free time are endangered species. That's why the bread machine is such a great tool: It saves our limited free time, and improves the quality of our lives with delicious, fresh, homemade bread. I rank bread machines right up alongside cordless power tools as one of the great tools of our time, and I would not live for long without one.

Like all tools, bread machines work best if operated knowledgeably. Owner's manuals and factory operating instructions are usually adequate, but they often gloss over, speed by, talk down, or even ignore rather than concentrate on helpful, practical information. Which is why this book is here.

Quite simply, the more you know, the better your bread will be. This book is a compilation of useful and relevant information about baking bread in bread machines, as well as bread making in general, distilled from years of experience and study. I have tried to be as honest and straightforward as possible. I hope that you'll find the information useful, and that it will help you turn out great breads.

So, gentlemen, start your machines!

PART I

Bread Machine Basics

CHAPTER 1

Ground Rules

*T*his chapter sets the ground rules for making bread in bread machines. Following them should make it easier for you to get what you want from this book.

Loaf Size

The recipes in this book are for one-pound loaves and one-and-a-half-pound loaves, roughly equivalent to loaves made from two or three cups of flour, respectively. If you don't know which size your machine makes, check the recipes that came with it. You can also figure loaf size by measuring out the number of cups of water your bread pan will hold. Pans that hold up to ten cups are one-pounders, those that hold up to fifteen cups are one-and-a-half-pounders, and pans that hold sixteen cups and up are two-pounders.*

Recipe Directions

I didn't want to insult your intelligence by repeating the same exact directions over and over, so you won't find basic directions for each recipe. I assume that you have at least paged through your instruction book and know the basics about your machine. I have included any unusual instructions, unique procedures, or special hints for a particular bread. Otherwise, load your machine and bake your bread according to the instructions that came with the machine.

What Order to Add Ingredients?

You should generally add liquid ingredients to the bread pan before the dry ones, and this is the order I have followed in the ingredients' lists with each recipe. But machines differ, so check the instruction book that came with your machine. If you are going to make a loaf immediately, it hardly matters how you add the ingredients. To use the delayed-start timer, however, it is important to keep the yeast away from the liquid. I usually add ingredients more or less according to the directions, and only take special care when I am going to set the timer.

Which Bread Setting to Use?

There are so many differences between machines that naming settings for each recipe could easily become confusing or even

*Not all machines can handle a two-pound loaf, so we have not included recipes for this size. Also, since homemade bread tends to get stale quickly, you have to eat a lot of bread fast to finish a two-pounder before it becomes inedible. When you want to make two-pound loaves, simply double the recipe for a one-pounder for all ingredients except the yeast. Rather than double the yeast, simply add an extra teaspoon.

useless. Also, if you like to "improve" recipes, your changes might require a different setting. The only way you'll know is if you understand what each setting is used for.

Regular/Basic/Normal/White Bread Setting

Use this setting for nearly any recipe that contains at least 50 percent white bread flour. Some machines also use this setting for whole wheat and whole grain breads.

Wheat/Whole Wheat Setting

Use this setting for recipes containing from 50 percent to 100 percent whole wheat or other whole grain flour.

Rapid Bake/Quick Bake Setting (Regular or Wheat)

Use this setting to make a loaf quickly. Machines generally have separate regular and wheat rapid cycles; choose your cycle according to the type of flour used. This setting generally requires the use of quick-rising yeast.

French/European Setting

Use this setting for recipes with little or no fat or sugar. It produces a dry loaf with an extra-crisp crust.

Sweet/Fruit and Nut/Raisin Bread Setting

Use this setting for recipes that contain a lot of sugar, or that require added ingredients during the kneading period. Some machines bake at a lower temperature on this setting to prevent the bread or added ingredients from burning. All machines will sound an audible alarm to indicate when you should add additional ingredients.

Dough Setting

Use this setting for recipes to be mixed and kneaded by the machine and then removed, formed by hand, and baked in a conventional oven.

Safety First

You're probably already aware of most of the following precautions, but since safe is better than sorry, we'll run through them again.

Don't use perishable ingredients when using the delayed-start timer. Sitting in the machine for hours waiting for the action to start can cause perishable ingredients to spoil, especially during warm weather.

Bread machines tend to crank it up into high gear while mixing and kneading, and as a result can vibrate and even "walk" a little. So keep your machine away from counter and table edges.

Bread machines generate considerable heat, so place them only on heat-resistant surfaces and move them away from the wall. The heat from a bread machine that's operated too close to a wall may discolor or otherwise damage the wall.

Do not operate your machine where it will be exposed to additional heat, such as in direct sunlight or next to or on a stove or oven. High temperatures can confuse and possibly scramble the machine's tiny brain, which has been programmed to keep the dough warm but has no way to cool it off.

Don't place anything on top of your machine while it is working—hot air and steam need to escape.

Stay away from the machine when it's working. The bread machine is a small oven that gets hot enough to cook your palm if you're not careful. Best to keep body parts away from the machine when it's warm, and use pot holders or towels to remove your steaming-hot bread when it finishes baking.

CHAPTER 2

Bread Machines

*T*en years ago, few could even imagine a bread-making machine. Today the machines are in millions of kitchens, and are considered by many to be a basic kitchen appliance, along with a stove and a refrigerator!

Basic Machine Features

Nearly everyone is making a bread machine these days, and many manufacturers are putting out entire lines of machines. Between the stripped-down economy models and the luxury models with the leather seats fall a whole range of machines, each sporting a unique list of features. Machine prices are obviously related to features, so use the following descriptions to determine which are of value to you. That way you may be able to avoid paying for features you'll never use.

Loaf Size

Bread machines bake one-, one-and-a-half-, or two-pound loaves. Before you make a purchase, remember that homemade bread has no preservatives and will stay fresh for only three to four days. Obviously, you don't want a lot of bread left on day five.

In addition, you can nearly always make smaller loaves than the rated size of your machine. If you have a one-and-a-half-pound machine, you also have a one-pounder. But you run the risk of giving your machine a hernia or overflowing your bread pan trying to make larger loaves than your machine is rated for. Definitely not a good idea!

Finally, you'll find yourself eating more bread with your own machine, simply because homemade is so darn good. In general, I'd recommend a one-and-a-half-pound machine for everyone except families with teenagers. Since teenagers never stop eating, two-pounders should easily disappear before they get stale.

Loaf Shape

Few machines turn out "conventional" or sandwich-shaped loaves. The most common shape available is the vertical rectangle, which is more or less like a short supermarket sandwich loaf stood on end. This loaf makes familiar-shaped slices when sliced from the side.

Other machines make round or cylindrical loaves. These are generally sliced in half from top to bottom, and then each half sliced from the side, producing half-rounds for sandwiches or to fit in a toaster. A few machines bake up loaves in a horizontal rectangle, which is similar to bread baked in a standard bread pan. Most bread lovers adapt easily to whatever shape their machine produces, although kids seem to prefer the familiar square shape for their sandwiches.

Preheat Cycle

Some machines pause before mixing to warm up the pan and ingredients. This saves you the trouble of bringing everything to room temperature before loading the pan, but does add extra time to the baking process. Many machines also pause at first when the whole wheat setting is used. This is to allow a little extra time for whole wheat flour to absorb liquid, since it tends to absorb it slowly.

Rapid Bake Cycle

Also referred to as Quick Bread, Quick Bake, or Turbo cycle, this feature produces bread in as little as two-and-a-half hours. This is nearly an hour shorter then the regular cycle, although some machines do complete their regular cycle in less than three hours. Most rapid bake cycles require quick-rising yeast, and produce shorter, denser, heavier loaves than regular cycles.

Dough Setting

This setting will mix and knead a dough, and allow it to rise before shutting off. You then remove the dough from the machine and form it by hand into breads, rolls, bagels, pretzels, pizzas, or whatever you wish. It's found on virtually all machines.

Whole Wheat Setting

Whole wheat breads are heavier and require longer kneading and rising times. Many machines include a whole wheat setting that will do just that.

French Bread Setting

French bread is made with reduced amounts of sugar and fat and requires longer rising and baking times. Machines with this setting turn out thick, crisp-crusted loaves with chewy centers.

Sweet Bread Setting

Sugar and fruit tend to burn easily, so some machines include a sweet bread setting that bakes at a lower temperature for a longer

time. You can also use this setting for breads that are high in fat,
or that contain cheese or other ingredients that burn easily.

Fruit-and-Nut Audible Alert

Because of the vigorous mixing and kneading action of most bread
machines, fruit or nuts added with the flour at the beginning of the
process will be pulverized beyond recognition. That's great for
spreading a flavor or color throughout the loaf, but not quite what
we had in mind for raisin bread! To avoid this, many machines will
sound an alert five to ten minutes before the kneading cycle
is complete, at which time you can add fruit and nuts. This allows
the ingredients to be completely mixed into the dough, but is
not long enough for the machine to chew up and digest them.

Delayed-Start Timer

The delayed-start timer is probably the most popular bread machine
feature because it allows you to program the machine to finish baking at a specified time. It's great when you want to wake up to a fresh
loaf of bread, or when you want a warm loaf at dinnertime. It's also
useful to keep bread from getting soggy in the machine after
baking; simply program the bread to finish baking when someone
will be at home to remove it. A standard feature on all machines.

Keep Warm or Cool-Down Cycle

Freshly baked bread will get soggy if it is not immediately removed
from the pan. To remedy this, many machines incorporate a cycle
that either continues to heat the baking chamber to help evaporate
the steam, or else turns on a fan to blow the hot moist air out of the
machine.

Crust Color Selector

Most machines allow you to bake bread to your preferred crust
color. The usual default is a medium color, which can produce

some very dark crusts on sweet breads, egg breads, or whole wheat breads. Choose the light setting to avoid this problem.

Viewing Window

Most machines have a viewing window that allows you to watch the entire bread-making process. A good idea in theory, especially since I find it far more interesting to watch the machine knead dough than most of what network TV has to offer these days (aside from sports). However, many viewing windows tend to be too small to be of value, and unless the machine is right under a light, it's often too dark inside the machine to see anything.

Cycle Indicators

As the machine advances through the entire bread-making process, some machines have indicators that tell what cycle the machine is in.

Power Saver

If the power goes off, or someone accidentally jerks the plug, you've lost your loaf—unless your machine has a power saver feature. The power saver enables the machine to restart right where it was interrupted, as long as the outage is short enough. Each machine has its own time limit for holding memory, so check your owner's manual for exact time limits. However, if the failure occurs while the bread is baking, your loaf is a goner. Throw in the towel and throw out the loaf.

Miscellaneous Settings

In an effort to make bread machines even more useful, manufacturers have come up with an interesting and slightly bizarre series of features. Machines will now also bake quick breads or cakes (using baking powder or soda rather than yeast), make

jam, cook rice, or even churn butter from cream! I admit that I
am neither an expert on nor a fan of most of the miscellaneous
features, but I can tell you that bread machines make bread better than they do anything else.

Personal Recommendations for Buying Bread Machines

Because of my obsession with bread machines, I am frequently
asked which machine is the best. I cannot answer that question
any more than I can tell you which car is the best. I could recommend a Lexus, which might be perfect for driving in Atlanta but
not the best for trekking around the wilds of Alaska. So rather
than looking for the best machine, you should study the available options and determine which are of value to you.

What I can do is list the features that I find useful, and tell
you what I know about the various models. Again, the more sophisticated the equipment, the higher the price. But in the end,
all bread machines, regardless of features or price, are capable of
making excellent bread. I have worked with all of the major
brand-name machines, and every single one of them has turned
out great bread. Naturally, I've had some embarrassing flops—
but that was my fault, not the machine's. So regardless of what
machine you get, you'll be able to turn out great bread.

My Favorite Features

Here is the short list of my favorite features.

Viewing window: I like a machine with viewing window—
preferably a large one. Although I frequently open the lid in the
early stages to check the dough and make necessary repairs, I
like being able to glance at the dough whenever I walk by, just
to make sure everything is okay. A window does prove very
handy at the end of the final rise, when an overactive dough
could be threatening to overflow the pan or push up against the
top. It's nice to see that you've got a potential disaster on your

hands before it actually occurs. (To dodge this disaster, open the lid and deflate the dough a bit by poking the top with a toothpick.)

Audible alert in multiple settings: Many machines include an audible alert, but some machines only sound the alert during a specific setting (for instance, the sweet bread setting), while others beep during most of their settings. Since I am fond of throwing all kinds of things into all kinds of bread, I prefer a machine that sounds the alert for all settings.

Baking cycle indicator: I'm not sure how critical this is to producing good bread, but it has kept me from popping open a lid during the baking stage on more than one occasion.

Clock: Several manufacturers have put clocks into their machines. Not just countdown timers, but actual clocks, along with the timers. I find this especially handy since I regularly use the delayed-timer feature to have my bread ready at a specific time.

Cool-down cycle: Despite any system to prevent it, bread will get damp if you leave it in the machine after baking. However, without a cool-down system, damp turns into wet. Thus any cool-down system is better than none at all. Of the two systems available, I think that a cooling fan is the most effective. So while I try not to let any loaf sit in the machine, for those that have to wait, I would rather they wait in a machine with a whirling fan.

Bread Machines

In the following notes, the information about features and capabilities is more important than model numbers, since the machines are still evolving and changing continuously. Models will change, but the features unique to each brand will be carried over from model to model. (Features common to all machines such as delayed-start timers and dough settings have not been listed.) I would like to thank all the manufacturers listed below for providing both equipment and assistance; without your help, this book could not have been written.

Betty Crocker Model BC1694: If you prefer conventionally shaped loaves, this is one of the machines that turns out a rectangular loaf similar to those baked in regular bread pans. It also uses forced air (convection) baking to shorten baking time and to assure an evenly baked loaf. Other features: two-pound capacity, time-of-day clock, no viewing window, E-Z Glide lid, rapid bake settings for white and wheat breads, cool-down fan, multisetting fruit-and-nut audible alert, and a kneading blade that reverses direction.

Black & Decker Model B-1600: Here's a familiar name to tool collectors. This is one of the few machines on the market that comes with a two-year warranty. It also features a unique triple-rise whole grain setting. Other features: two-pound capacity, large viewing window, crust color control, rapid bake setting for white bread, cool-down cycle, multisetting fruit-and-nut audible alert, and an instructional video.

Breadman Model TR-500: One of the fastest machines on the market, the Breadman will bake a loaf of wheat bread in as little as two hours and twenty minutes. This is not a rapid bake feature, but the regular baking setting. Other features: one-and-a-half-pound capacity, cool-down cycle, multisetting fruit-and-nut audible alert, and an instructional video.

Breadman Ultra Model TR-700: The Ultra also features short baking times, even though it has a larger capacity. A two-pound loaf can be finished in as little as two hours and fifty minutes. Other features: two-pound capacity, large viewing window, rapid bake setting for wheat bread, cake and jam settings, cool-down cycle, multisetting fruit-and-nut audible alert, and an instructional video.

Hitachi Model HB-D102: Pizza lovers will like the pizza dough cycle on this machine. This cycle has been specially programmed with two rising periods to produce pizza dough. Other features: one-and-a-half-pound capacity, rapid bake setting for white bread, cake setting, cool-down fan, and a multisetting fruit-and-nut audible alert.

Oster Model 4811: The cast aluminum bread pan on this model is the most substantial pan that I've ever seen on a bread machine. It produces bread with thick, crisp crusts; the French bread is wonderful. Other features on this quiet running machine: one-and-a-half-pound capacity, crust color control, bake cycle indicators, rapid bake setting for white and wheat breads, cool-down cycle, multisetting fruit-and-nut audible alert, and a two-year warranty.

Panasonic Model SD-YD150: This model is unique in that it has a yeast dispenser. Rather than adding yeast to the bread pan, you pour it into the dispenser and the machine automatically adds it at the proper time. Other features: one-and-a-half-pound capacity, no viewing window, rectangular cast aluminum bread pan, sandwich bread baking mode, rapid bake setting for white and wheat breads, cool-down cycle, and a multisetting fruit-and-nut audible alert.

Regal Model K6750: If this model loses power while making a loaf of bread, it will automatically resume operation if power is restored within two minutes. It will also bake a loaf on a regular baking setting in as little as two hours and forty minutes. Other features: one-and-a-half-pound capacity, crust color control, bake cycle indicators, rapid bake setting for white bread, quick bread, jam, and rice setting, cool-down cycle, multisetting fruit-and-nut audible alert, and an instructional video.

Toastmaster Model 1195: Not only will this machine bake your bread, it will also churn butter from heavy whipping cream. A plastic lid keeps the cream in the pan during the thirty-minute butter cycle. Other features: two-pound capacity, large viewing window, regular white bread cycles under three hours, rapid bake setting for wheat bread, cool-down cycle, and multisetting fruit-and-nut audible alert.

West Bend Model 41040: This is the only bread machine that I know of that is made in the U.S.A. It also features a unique lock setting to prevent any accidental interference with the control buttons after the machine has been turned on. Other features: one-and-a-half-pound capacity, removable cover with large viewing window, crust color control, bake cycle indicators, rapid bake setting for white and wheat breads, cool-down cycle, and an instructional video.

Zojirushi Model BBCC-S15A: This quiet-running machine is for serious bread makers. Users have the option of programming the entire bread-making sequence, along with a complete selection of pre-programmed cycles. Other features: one-and-a-half-pound capacity, time-of-day clock, large viewing window, crust color control, bake cycle indicators, quick baking setting for white bread, cake and jam settings, cool-down fan, timer that shows the time of completion rather than the duration of the process, kneading rod in the side of baking pan, and a kneading blade that reverses direction.

Care

Caring for your machine basically amounts to keeping it clean. Operating instructions that come with the machines go into great detail about cleaning this and soaking that and who knows what else. But really, only a few points are worth remembering.

First, if you don't clean out the bread pan between loaves, your bread will take on some "interesting" tastes and textures from past loaves. I generally just take a dish towel and wipe out the pan. If any bread has stuck to or under the mixing paddle, I just set the pan aside for a while, let the bread get brittle dry, and then crush it and dump it out.

Quite often the mixing paddle will stick in the pan, which calls for soaking in water to remove. I usually don't bother. It's right where it belongs, and if it doesn't come out, I won't lose it. If it looks like I'm not getting the pan clean down around the paddle, I will occasionally resort to soaking just so that I can give it a good cleaning.

Never submerge your bread pan in water to clean it. If you really must use soap and water on it, you can fill the pan and wash the whole thing, but keep the bottom of the pan out of water. There are bearings and lubricants around the drive shaft that could be destroyed by water.

Because the bread pan and mixing paddle are coated with nonstick material, it's not a good idea to use a crowbar on loaves that are hard to get out. In fact, any metal and most sharp or pointed tools will damage the coating. And a damaged coating means that loaves will be even harder to remove. Best just to shake the pan vigorously, or whack it a few times with your palm. In severe cases, invert the pan and knock the edge sharply against a breadboard.

Likewise for the mixing paddle when it sticks in a loaf of bread. Use a chopstick or other wooden tool to remove it, rather than an ice pick or paring knife, and you'll avoid some cleaning headaches.

Over time, crumbs and flour will accumulate inside the baking chamber of the machine. If you let it go for too long, you'll be reminded by a little smoke and some obnoxious odors. So it pays to occasionally stick a sponge into the machine and clean out all the miscellaneous debris.

Since I like to eyeball working loaves whenever I happen to pass by, I try to keep the viewing window clean. But I stay away from commercial glass cleaners because the high heat of the machine can generate some nasty fumes off their residue. Water works the best. That goes for the inside of the machine as well; clean it with water and leave the Lime-Away for the bathroom.

Repair

Years back, when moderately skilled handymen could actually tune up their own cars, most household machines were mechanical devices that could be opened up and sometimes even successfully repaired at home. The good news/bad news of the 90s is that most equipment works better and costs less than it used to, but is far too complex for the common man to comprehend, much less repair.

Bread machines fall into that category. In fact, they are among the more complex home appliances. They rank up there with microwaves, far past toaster technology. For that reason, it is generally not a good idea to strap on the old tool belt and start dismantling an indisposed bread machine. Even your local appliance repairman would be hard pressed to repair a bread machine. This is why a number of manufacturers recommend returning sick machines directly to them, rather than taking it to one of their local authorized repair centers.

Another reason, according to well-known service technician Robert Dillingham, is that few bread machines ever develop problems. The failure rate is so low that it simply does not justify training a whole repair network. Robert has spent years tearing down and repairing every machine on the market, and has not only written about bread machines, but has also served as a consultant for several manufacturers, as well as for *Consumer Reports*. Robert's knowledge is extensive, and his advice is well worth following.

Robert agrees that it's a bit foolhardy to attempt home repairs on a misbehaving bread machine, especially since the circuit board is so easily damaged by static electricity. Without the proper equipment, you may zap your machine's brain. He advises those who suspect a problem to go back to the beginning and try making a plain and simple loaf of white bread. Don't judge your machine's health by trying a heavy, whole grain loaf, which can be difficult even under ideal conditions.

Test your machine with the simplest loaf you know will work. That should tell you whether your machine is at fault or not. If the machine bakes up a nice white loaf, then it's time to look for other reasons for your low success rate. Robert says that callers often tell him that they think their machine is defective because two or three loaves out of five fail. "If the machine wasn't working," Robert says, "the failure rate would be five out of five."

The most frequent problem, according to Robert, is stretching of the drive belt. Like the belts in your car, the one in the bread maker will stretch as it gets old, resulting in under-kneaded dough that produces loaves that gradually get shorter and shorter. The bread machine chef often doesn't realize that his loaves are slowly getting shorter until a neighbor or friend remarks that "this loaf is smaller than the last one you gave me."

Robert told me that changing a belt on some machines is a simple five-minute job. Unfortunately, many other machines require a total tear-down, which rules out anyone but a trained technician. And then, some manufacturers will sell parts like belts to consumers, while others will not. You're probably better off just letting the experts handle this, as well as other repairs.

The second biggest problem that Robert encounters is a blown thermal sensor. This little device works like a fuse, tripping when the temperature in the machine reaches a certain level to keep the machine from bursting into flame and burning down the house. Unfortunately, it cannot be reset but must instead be replaced. And again, even though we may be talking about a $2 part, this is not a job for amateurs. Robert says that the problem often occurs when successive loaves are baked and the sensor doesn't get a chance to cool down, or else when the machine is in a location that receives extra heat, such as under a heat vent or in direct sunlight.

One last piece of advice that Robert urged me to pass along involves setting the delayed timer. He said that in his experience, most loaves baked using the timer tend to be a bit dry. Unfortunately, the drier the dough, the greater the workload for the machine, which can lead to all kinds of problems. If you notice that loaves baked using the timer tend to be a bit dry, be nice to your machine and add a little extra liquid at the start. Your machine will appreciate the reduced workload, and will be more likely to die of old age rather than a heart attack.

Myth Bashing

Before we get any further down the road, I'd like to put an end to a number of bread machine misconceptions that don't have the decency to die and stay dead. All of these so-called truths are discussed in more detail elsewhere in this book; for now, just take my word for it.

Good loaves fill the bread pan. Nonsense! Just take a look around your local bakery and see the incredible variation in size.

Different breads have different qualities, and those differing qualities determine the size and shape of the loaf. Our goal is great-tasting bread; size is irrelevant.

A recipe will bake up the same every time it is used. Nice if it were true. Sorry to say that due to numerous conditions beyond our control, it's possible to try the same recipe on five consecutive days and come up with five different loaves.

Because bread machines are very forgiving, careful measurement is a waste of time. Forgiving is not a word I would use to describe bread machines, especially when talking about liquid-to-flour ratios. While it may not matter how many raisins you throw in for a loaf of raisin bread, if you're a cup off in your liquid or flour measurement, I can guarantee that your attitude will be anything but forgiving when you view the end results.

Good breads are light and airy with smooth sides and a nice rounded top. I'm not after light and airy when I make a rye or cheese loaf. I'm looking for flavor. Texture, size, and shape will vary according to ingredients. A slightly sunken or gnarled top doesn't by itself indicate a failed loaf, likewise for a dense chewy texture. Let your taste buds, not your eyes, be the judge.

Just add the ingredients, press start, and come back later for a perfect loaf of bread. This can and does occasionally happen, but most recipes can use a little help from their friends. Especially new recipes. There are simply too many variables out there for all recipes to work perfectly in your machine.

Bread machines are hard to use and produce second-rate bread. Here's a news flash for whiners: All sophisticated tools require knowledgeable users to produce positive results. Using a bread machine requires the use of a functioning brain. Those unwilling to learn a few basics, and then apply them knowledgeably, are sure to turn out unpalatable bread in their hard-to-use machines. Those who take the time to learn and apply their knowledge can easily produce masterpieces.

Reality Check

Like grilling or barbecuing, baking bread in a machine is far from an exact science. In both cases, adjustments must be made for conditions that exist at that particular time. For instance, instructions that call for grilling a T-bone steak for three minutes per side will not always turn out an outstanding steak. Grilling a perfect steak requires taking into account the thickness of the meat, the fat content, the moisture content, the heat of the fire, and more.

Likewise for baking bread. The fact is that bread machines do not automatically turn out perfect loaves every time. Many variables beyond our control affect the outcome of each and every loaf, and the only sure way to produce consistently good bread is to learn a bit about the process. Fortunately, this is an enjoyable process with a short learning curve.

So don't be discouraged if your success rate is low when you first start, you're just like everyone else. All the information you need to become a bread machine chef is here. Once you've learned a few basics about both your machine and bread making in general, you're going to start turning out great breads. And once you've got it, you'll keep it. Making great bread will become a normal part of your life.

CHAPTER 3

Ingredients

*B*uilding a loaf of bread is like any other construction job: The finished product is only as good as the materials or ingredients that go into it. So to build a great loaf of bread, we need to know something about the ingredients. This chapter includes basic information about the ingredients necessary for making bread, as well as some possible consequences of using either too much or too little of the more important ingredients.

Basic Ingredients

Almost all breads are made from the same basic ingredients. Knowing the role that each of these play gives you a solid foundation that will result in great loaves of bread.

Yeast

Bread yeast is a simple-minded, single-celled fungus that produces carbon dioxide bubbles and alcohol when it contacts warm liquids and food (flour and sugar in this case). The bubbles then get trapped by the gluten in the dough and cause it to rise, while the alcohol is burned off by baking.

Yeast is available in several different forms. The yeast to use in bread machines is called active dry yeast. Compressed yeast cakes and quick-rising yeast don't seem to work as well or produce as consistently. (I've also tried beer yeasts, and have produced only nasty tasting bread.)

Active dry yeast is available in individual quarter-ounce packets or in bulk amounts. With a bread machine, you are going to find yourself making a lot of bread, and those little packets of yeast will quickly become a nuisance, as well as expensive! So buy in bulk.

Supermarkets carry a money-saving four-ounce jar that is the equivalent of about sixteen packets. Larger quantities are generally available at natural food stores, which often have bulk yeast available. Local warehouse discounters generally carry a two-pound bag that will save you some serious money. I buy the two-pounders to refill a four-ounce jar that I use every time I make bread. I keep the balance tightly sealed and stored in the frig.

Fleischmann's and Red Star are the two major yeast makers, and they're both available nearly everywhere. This is not a scientific opinion, but I can't really find any difference between them at all! Basically, they both work well, and they work every time.

Downside: Not enough yeast will turn out short, heavy, dense loaves that look like squared-off hockey pucks on steroids. As an average, you need to add from one to two-and-a-half teaspoons per loaf (quarter-ounce supermarket packets contain just under 2½ teaspoons.)

Too much yeast can cause a number of problems. An absurd excess can produce enough alcohol to pickle itself, resulting in an inedible, collapsed loaf. A simple excess of yeast will cause the dough to rise and rise and rise. If you're lucky, the loaf will just rise high above the pan and bake without burning or sticking to anything. It is likely to have an overly strong yeast flavor, and be very airy, with perhaps more holes than bread.

If you're not so lucky, the dough will rise up, stick to the top of the machine, and probably mushroom out over the edges of the pan. This will produce a loaf that is glued to the top of the machine and burned around the mushroom top. Aside from filling your kitchen full of smoke and setting off the smoke alarm, these hyperactive loaves are a nightmare to clean out of the machine. Plan on cleaning for an hour or four.

Liquids

Liquids are essential. They revive the yeast and activate the gluten.

Just about anything edible that more-or-less pours can be used as a liquid, including water, milk, buttermilk, yogurt, sour cream, fruit or vegetable juices, cottage cheese, beer, soup, coffee, and so on. Treated water will not help your bread; in fact, it can literally prevent you from turning out tall, handsome, delicious loaves. If you live in a metropolitan area, your water is treated. Do yourself a favor and try making some bread with bottled water; you could be in for a pleasant surprise.

Milk or milk products, in either a liquid or dry form, produce a rich, fine-grained bread with a softer crust. They also add nutrients and flavor, and improve color and shelf-life. Water produces a coarser-grained bread with a crisp crust.

Liquid temperature is critical: too cold and the yeast will ignore the wake-up call, too hot and it'll boil. But you don't need a digital thermometer to check the temperature because body temperature is just about perfect, meaning that the liquid will feel neutral on your finger, neither hot nor cold.

Downside: Without enough liquid, bread dough will be too hard and firm to rise, resulting in a dense, heavy, inedible loaf. Too much liquid can cause dough to rise so high it collapses.

Sugar/Sweetener

Sugar feeds the yeast, adds flavor and sweetness, and makes a tender bread with a fine texture. It also helps to brown the crust and increases edible life by retaining moisture.

Other acceptable sweeteners include brown sugar, molasses, corn syrup, honey, maple syrup, and malt syrup or powder. All may be used interchangeably, although when using liquid sweeteners, be sure to adjust the amount of liquid in the recipe. (Reduce the liquid by one-third the amount of liquid sweetener added. So if you substitute three tablespoons of honey for sugar, reduce the liquid by one tablespoon.)

Molasses, used primarily for dark breads, is available either sulfured or unsulfured. Unsulfured has a less bitter flavor; use either interchangeably.

Warning: Artificial sweeteners will "die" when subjected to high heat, and therefore should not be used. Confectioners' sugar contains cornstarch, so avoid it.

Downside: Too little sweetener will restrict yeast activity, resulting in a smaller, less-sweet loaf with a pale crust. Overdosing your bread with sugar will rob the dough of liquid, which will produce a squat, heavy loaf with a dark or blackened crust.

Salt

Salt makes bread taste better. It also helps control the yeast and strengthens the gluten and allows it to behave correctly.

Downside: Bread made without salt will lack flavor, have a coarse, open texture, and may over-rise and collapse. Too much salt will interfere with yeast activity, producing a bitter, salty tasting loaf that will not rise.

Fat

Fat tenderizes and softens the texture of bread, and increases moisture and richness. It also adds flavor and helps to keep bread fresh. Butter, lard, margarine, oil, and shortening may all be used interchangeably in bread making, but obviously each will add a slightly different flavor. Whipped, light, and other specialty margarines do not work well, so forget 'em.

Several points to keep in mind about fats: Butter and buttery-tasting margarines contribute a buttery taste and a yellow color to breads that will be lost if other fats are used. Lard, infrequently used and definitely an ingredient non grata in these health-conscious days, is the flavor champion in the fat category; use it if you dare for great flavor, especially in heavier, whole-grain breads.

Also, since fat in excess amounts actually works against the gluten (that's where the name shortening came from—it breaks or shortens long gluten strands into shorter units), it's important to limit the amount in one-pound recipes to no more than one-quarter cup, and in one-and-a-half-pound recipes to no more than one-third cup.

Downside: Bread without enough fat will have less flavor, a coarser texture, and a very short edible life. Too much fat will limit rising power and produce squat loaves.

Gluten

Found only in wheat grain and, in small amounts, in rye grain, gluten is what enables dough to rise. When water is added to flour, gluten particles become elastic, sticky, and strong. Kneading brings these sticky particles in contact with each other, where they'll stick together like they've been super-glued. Once stuck together, they'll form long continuous strands that then trap the carbon dioxide bubbles.

Gluten also gives bread the strength to hold together and stand tall. When the dough is baked, the gluten solidifies and becomes the supporting structure of the loaf.

You can buy packages of gluten at natural food stores or by mail order. Added in small amounts (approximately 1 tablespoon per cup of flour) to whole grain doughs, gluten can turn small, heavy, dense rocks into tall, finely textured loaves.

Although gluten is available under a variety of names and concentrations, I use the term "vital gluten" throughout this book. This is a gluten that is approximately 75 percent pure protein. Adjust accordingly if the gluten you use is a different percentage.

Downside: Too little gluten will produce small, lead-like tooth-busters that have little resemblance to bread. An excess of gluten might produce a handsome loaf, but it would taste like dirty socks.

Flour

Flour's flour, right? These days, we all know that nothing's that simple any more, but since all we're trying to do is make some great bread, I'm going to skip over why you don't want flour made from wheat grown in either the humid central states or from the Northwest, and simply advise you to use flour labeled "bread flour." These white and wheat flours are milled from combinations of wheats that contain large amounts of gluten. The key here is gluten, without which bread would have the consistency of dry old clods of dirt.

An amazing number of products come from wheat grains, including all-purpose flour, bread flour, wheat or whole wheat flour, pastry flour, cake flour, wheat germ, cracked wheat, rolled wheat flakes, and more. Although any of these may be used in making bread, I highly recommend that you start with bread flour for recognizable flavors and shapes.

In addition, you can use many other flours or grain products to make bread. These include amaranth, barley, cornmeal, buckwheat, millet, oats, quinoa, rice, rye, soy, triticale, and more. Any of these may be substituted for bread flour as long as bread flour is at least 50 percent of the flour used. As a rule of thumb, when I experiment, I never use less than two-thirds bread flour on my first try. Results are generally edible, and the recipe is easily adjusted from that point.

One last point about mixing flours. Generally speaking, any variation from 100 percent bread flour will produce a smaller, denser loaf. This is natural, since less gluten means less ability to "get it up." This doesn't mean that the bread is no good; it may be delicious but small. For instance, nobody expects a heavy bread like pumpernickel to bake up as high as a loaf of white bread. So don't just toss your short loaves over the fence hoping to choke the idiot barking dog next door, let 'em cool and try a piece. You may have baked up a heavy little masterpiece!

There are several brands of bread flour on supermarket shelves these days, and I'm sure they're all good. However, years ago I started using Gold Medal Better for Bread bread flour and liked the results. Since it has never let me down, I continue to use and recommend it to this day, and, in fact, all recipes in this book were tested using Better for Bread flour.

Downside: Too little flour will produce a damp dough and a finished loaf that remains raw in the center. Too much flour will result in a hard dough and a dense, heavy loaf.

Eggs

Eggs, while by no means essential to bread making, add color, flavor, and a rich, cake-like texture. Breads made with eggs will also keep longer. Recipes that call for eggs always refer to USDA large eggs; you can also substitute three small eggs for two large eggs. You can use egg substitutes in place of eggs—in fact, they're easier to use if a recipe calls for half an egg.

If you're adding eggs to an existing recipe, remember to reduce the amount of liquid. I find that a straight ounce-for-ounce substitution leaves the dough a bit dry, so I reduce the liquid by half of the amount of egg that I am adding. For instance, since a large egg equals about four ounces, if I add one egg to a recipe, I decrease the liquid about two ounces.

Who's Who in Grains and Flours

Yeast breads always start with a base of wheat flour because of the gluten that it contains; from that point on, any available grain or flour may be added. Obviously, different grains, flours, and combinations thereof will produce totally different results. Regardless, the following should help explain just what all these grains and flours are.

Wheat

Wheat is the leading cereal (meaning edible) grain in the world, and most of the flour in our supermarkets comes from the wheat grain. There are, however, a number of different flours that are milled from the wheat grain.

All-purpose flour is a super-refined mixture of high- and low-gluten grains. Because it loses most of its vitamins and nutrients in the milling process, it commonly has those elements added back and is known as *enriched*. *Bleached flour* has been chemically whitened, while *unbleached* has been allowed to age and whiten without help from chemists.

Bread flour is milled from high-gluten, hard, red spring wheat kernels, and will produce high-rising, light, flavorful loaves of bread. Supermarket varieties are also enriched and often contain a dough conditioner such as ascorbic acid (Vitamin C), which helps strengthen the dough.

Whole wheat flour is ground from the entire wheat berry, which includes the bran and germ. Bran is the outer shell of the berry and is mainly indigestible cellulose fiber—no nutrition, but good roughage. Wheat germ is loaded nutritionally, so whole wheat flour is not enriched. Because wheat germ contains oil, whole wheat flour can turn rancid, and therefore should be stored in a refrigerator and used within six months. Bran (both wheat and oat bran) and wheat germ may be purchased individually for use in bread making.

Graham flour, or cracked wheat, is coarsely ground whole wheat flour. Although it supplies bread with an "unshaved" character, a chewy texture, and strong flavor, it should be used in moderation since the sharp-edged flour particles can cut the strands of gluten, resulting in a small, heavy, really chewy loaf.

Pastry flour is milled from low-gluten soft wheat, and is used primarily for cakes and pastries. Generally considered unsuitable for bread baking, it produces a tight crumb and soft texture if added in small quantities to bread flour.

Semolina or **durum flour** is made from durum wheat berries, the hardest wheat variety, and is almost exclusively used for making pasta. Adding a small amount to bread flour produces an Italian or Mediterranean flavored bread.

Self-rising or instant-blending flours have their uses, but not for bread!

Other Grains

As our world continues to shrink, more and more new foods are finding their way into our supermarkets and homes. Some of the names in the listing below are old friends, although you may not know them as bread-making ingredients, while others are total strangers. All can be used for bread making; but since none of them contain any appreciable amount of gluten, add them to bread recipes in small quantities to add flavor, texture, or color.

Amaranth: A tiny, golden grain commonly known as the Aztec grain. Use the cooked grain or amaranth flakes or flour to add a strong earthy flavor to breads.

Barley: A familiar, sweet, and mildly nutty flavored grain that can be used in several forms for bread making: flakes, flour, or barley malt. The flakes and flour are low gluten and must be used with a high-gluten flour. Barley malt, often sold as diastatic malt powder, is a sweetener that will add flavor and height to breads.

Buckwheat: Technically a seed rather than a grain, buckwheat makes flour that is a strongly flavored and extremely popular addition to pancakes. A small amount of buckwheat flour (one-quarter cup) in a bread recipe produces a delicious, distinctive flavored loaf.

Corn: Available in many colors and a variety of grinds, cornmeal is used for corn breads and in Mexican and Southwestern cooking. Cornmeal or corn flour adds a unique, distinctive flavor and a crumbly, slightly rough texture to breads. Limit cornmeal to under one-half cup in bread recipes.

Millet: Tiny millet grains, which may be added without cooking, add a crunch and a slightly bitter flavor to breads; millet flour is also available.

Oats: Oats are available in several forms useful for bread making. The best known is rolled oats—oatmeal. You can add rolled oats, oat flour, or oat meal directly to bread recipes.

Quinoa: Originally grown only in Peru, this nutty flavored, multicolored, tiny grain can be used whole, without cooking; also available as flour.

Rye: A popular and familiar bread ingredient, rye is used in many forms. The rye berry can be sprouted and used whole, or it may be milled into a number of different grinds. Cracked rye, the coarsest grind available, is the rye equivalent of cracked wheat. Rye meal, or pumpernickel, is the next coarsest grind; it is used to create dark, almost black, chewy loaves of rye bread. Rye flour is the finest grind, and varies in color from light to medium brown, depending on how much of the bran has been left in.

Teff: This microscopic, relatively unknown grain is ground to flour that adds considerable flavor to breads. Some claim it is better used in non-yeast items such as pancakes, waffles, and muffins.

Triticale: Triticale is the result of crossing rye with wheat, and has a slight sour flavor, similar to rye. Not as productive as hoped, triticale remains a minor crop, making the flour a bit pricey.

Grind Your Own

Grinding your own flour from wheat berries may seem a bit extreme until you taste the results. Freshly ground flour gives bread a sweet but robust flavor. No question about it: If your taste buds still work, you'll love the taste. However, if you're lucky enough to be buying from a local mill, there's no reason even to consider grinding your own.

When you grind up wheat berries, you get whole wheat flour. It can go rancid, so use the flour at once or refrigerate it to preserve the flavor. One cup of berries will yield about one-and-three-quarters cups of medium-fine ground flour. A pound of berries will produce about four-and-a-half cups of flour.

Don't even try to grind white bread flour at home. To do so, you'd first have to remove the bran and germ from the wheat berry.

You can grind your own flour with a number of different tools. Each will grind wheat berries into flour, but they all work differently, and the process ranges from a quiet, but strenuous workout to an eardrum-rattling walk in the park. Here are a few machines you might consider.

Vita-Mix Machines

If you own a Vita-Mix machine, you already have a grain-grinding machine. My maxi-4000 does a fair to middling job of grinding, with a minimum of effort. Ear plugs are a big help, and flipping the forward/reverse switch back and forth does take some time. After grinding for a bit, I generally dump the flour into a sifter, sift out the fine flour, and dump the coarser pieces back into the machine for more grinding. Large amounts of flour require large amounts of time. I wouldn't recommend buying a Vita-Mix as a flour grinder, especially since they're expensive. Well worth the money for the world's best blender, but hardly the world's best grain grinder.

Hand Grain Mills

Hand mills are quiet and easy to use, but they are a workout! Grinding flour is as simple as pouring in the wheat berries and turning the crank. Most machines have several settings so that you can grind both fine and coarse flours, although I have to run the flour through my grinder twice to get an even and consistent fine grind. The hand-cranker that I use is an Italian model with steel rollers and a knob that varies the distance between the rollers. Setting the rollers close together produces a fine flour, while at the other extreme, the wheat berries just get broken in half.

Although it's quiet and works well, the main problems with the grinder are the time involved and the muscle power required. Also, you have to set up the machine, clamp it down, and then tear it down and clean it when the fun of cranking finally finishes. Price range runs from $60 to $100 for a good quality grinder.

Electric Grain Mills

Electric mills are the ultimate in ease but they tend to be on the noisy side—and that's putting it mildly. Simply pour in the grain, pick the desired setting, insert ear plugs, and grind away. You can grind large quantities of flour quickly, making it possible to use on a regular basis. All the models that I've seen have good-sized motors with stainless steel milling heads that will easily grind grains (and beans) into everything from fine-grained pastry flour all the way to cracked grains or flakes. One major drawback is the physical size of these machines; I simply haven't got room to store one. And the other stumbling block is the price, around $250.

KitchenAid Grain Grinding Attachment

KitchenAid, the current kitchen mixer of choice, has a grinding accessory that attaches easily and quickly to the mixer. An infinitely adjustable knob allows you to grind a full range of flours quickly with virtually no effort and little noise. Since the grinder is an attachment, it gets put away after use but is within reach whenever needed. In addition to grains, it will also grind beans, corn, and any other non-oily product. Lives up to the KitchenAid reputation. Price runs from $100 to $150, depending on where you buy it.

CHAPTER 4

Bread-Making Techniques

Now that we've learned about machines and ingredients, it's about time to make some bread! This chapter contains all the information you need to make some great bread. Since bread machines can be ill-tempered and spiteful if ingredient quantities aren't close to perfect, we'll start with a short discussion about measuring those ingredients.

Measuring Ingredients

Bread machines have no sense of humor when it comes to measuring ingredients. A teaspoon more or less of water can turn a great loaf into a disaster, so I wouldn't recommend using your coffee cup as a measuring cup, or a soup spoon as a measuring spoon. Building a great loaf of bread is like any other job: To do it right, you need to use the right tools.

To measure liquids, use a clear glass or plastic measuring cup—a one-and-a-half- to two-cup capacity is a good size for bread making. Placing the cup on a level surface and reading the contents at eye-level is the only way to guarantee accuracy; "close enough for government work" will produce bread even less edible than our unbalanced federal budget. Opaque plastic and metal measuring cups are made to measure dry ingredients and will not measure liquids accurately.

Always level off dry ingredients to insure accuracy. To measure flour, spoon or scoop the flour into a cup until it overflows, then use a spatula, knife, or other straight-edged tool to scrape off the extra, leaving an exact amount. Don't dip the measuring cup into the flour, because that can pack it down, and considerably more than the required amount may end up in the cup. (Bread flour is presifted, and packing it into measuring cups just defeats this handy feature.)

Some ingredients should *always* be packed into measuring cups and spoons to insure accurate measurement: brown sugar, and all fats—including butter, margarine, shortening, and lard.

Most ingredients, however, should *never* be packed into measuring cups or spoons, including flour (see above) and grated cheese. To measure properly, spoon the cheese into the cup, filling the cup without tamping it down.

To measure small amounts of dry ingredients, invest in a good set of measuring spoons. I prefer the deeper, almost circular, stainless steel sets because they are easier to measure with and simple to clean. More expensive, sure, like most good tools. A set that contains a half-tablespoon is hard to find, but is a real time saver. To measure out small amounts, just dip the measuring spoons into the dry ingredient, and level off with a knife or another straight-edged tool.

Small quantities of liquids such as water, honey, and molasses are also measured in measuring spoons. No need to level these off; just fill the spoon full, without overflowing. To avoid mis-measuring or having to wash and dry measuring spoons, I have two sets for my bread making: one used only for dry ingredients, the other for wet.

The most important part of measuring ingredients is consistency. Always do it the same way with the same tools and you'll be able to repeat your results time after time. It hardly matters what you use to measure with as long as you can do it exactly the same way again. Unless, of course, you're following somebody else's recipe, in which case it comes in real handy to use standard measuring cups and spoons.

Baking Bread in Bread Machines

Although our goal is a perfect loaf every time we bake, the truth is that it's just not always going to happen. There are many reasons why, including measurement variations, the current temperature, the relative humidity, the altitude, the brand and type of flour, the region of the country, and more, but the main reason is the flour.

Because it is hygroscopic, meaning that it absorbs moisture from the air, flour can change from day to day along with the weather. In hot, dry weather, flour will contain little or no water, while in rainy or humid weather, the flour will actually absorb significant amounts. This can easily throw the liquid-to-flour ratio off enough to produce unattractive, inedible loaves. Other factors affecting the bread include the kind and grind of flour, the form and condition of the yeast, the number of kneading and rising cycles and the time of each, and the baking conditions.

So how do you get your machine to turn out excellent bread on a consistent basis? The answer is relatively simple: Get on a first-name basis with your machine and learn what proper dough looks and feels like. Getting to know your machine is the fast and easy part. All you need is about five minutes to learn how to work the control panel and figure out how the bread pan fits into the machine.

You also need to learn to diagnose problems from the assorted noises and sounds the machine makes, and that'll become second nature after the first dozen loaves of bread. Just as you automatically listen for problems every time you start your car, you'll learn to keep your ears tuned for the first few minutes whenever you put your bread machine to work.

Learning About Dough

Learning about bread dough is the slow and easy part. Ideally, after the dough has kneaded for a while, you want to see a ball that is smooth, soft, shiny, and a bit tacky. When the kneading finishes, the ball should sag a little, and slowly slump down onto the bottom and out toward the corners of the pan. Just get into the habit of eyeballing the dough after the first four or five minutes of kneading and making any necessary repairs, and you'll start producing great breads on a consistent basis. (See "Five-Minute Dough Check," below.)

To get a good look at the dough, forget the window and just pop open the lid. Opening the lid occasionally during the mixing and kneading stages is not a problem, although it's not a good idea to leave it open for extended periods. (Beyond the knead cycle, you risk your loaf by opening the top.) If the machine sounds okay, and everything looks okay, but you're still unsure, get technical and poke the dough.

Sticking your finger down into the kneading blade isn't the smartest move you'll ever make, but it's a simple matter to carefully poke the dough without risking a finger. This will tell you immediately what state your dough is in; it should feel soft and pliable and a little tacky, without being wet or sticky. If it's sticky, it needs more flour; if it's firm and hard, it needs more liquid.

Dough Differences

Naturally, not all doughs will behave the same. For instance, a dough made with cottage cheese will look very dry after the first few minutes of mixing. If you add liquid, you will probably ruin the bread: As the dough is mixed and kneaded, the cottage cheese will continue to be liquefied and mixed in, automatically adding the correct amount of liquid to the dough.

Another example is a dough to which you added moist fruit. Initially, this dough might also appear too dry; but when the fruit is finally broken down, it will add the required liquid.

So before you add anything to any dough, give a quick thought to the ingredients, especially if anything unusual has been included.

Dough Repairs

On the other hand, if you're making a more-or-less normal loaf of bread, trust your judgment and add ingredients at will. Add slowly; a tablespoon at a time is a good rate. Be sure to wait a couple of minutes before adding more because the dough takes some time to adjust.

Be careful, however, because tossing in a whole tablespoon at once can result in some of the material being thrown back out of the pan. So add slowly and allow the dough to absorb the additional material rather than toss it all over the machine. Occasionally, it seems to take forever to get the dough to the proper state. In that case simply turn off the machine and start it again to insure that the dough gets properly kneaded.

Five-Minute Dough Check

As you will read numerous times in this book, baby-sitting your machine for the first five to ten minutes is the best and perhaps only way you can guarantee yourself consistently great bread. As you make more and more bread, it'll become second nature to pop open the lid, repair the dough if necessary, and come back later to a great loaf. Listed below are some ailing dough conditions and suggested repairs. Be sure to note any additions on your recipe for future reference.

Pancake batter rather than bread dough: Either the recipe is worthless, or you miscounted and the dough is short a cup of flour. Solution: Throw in a cup of flour to start and keep your eye on it. Add more as needed.

Wet and stringy dough: The liquid-to-flour ratio is way off, assuming that all required ingredients were added. Solution: Add more flour. Start with a couple of tablespoons and watch. Add more as needed.

A ball forms, but it's real sticky and not smooth: A normal day, except that something's different—like the temperature or humidity—and the dough's a bit too damp. Solution: A tablespoon of flour should solve the problem. If one tablespoon doesn't seem to make much of a difference, try another. Then add by the teaspoon. Go slowly, you'll get it.

The dough sticks together but won't form a ball: Generally indicates a dough that's a bit dry, especially if the mass is jagged and irregular and pieces tend to tear off as it kneads. Solution: Add liquid, by the tablespoon at first, then by the teaspoon. Give the dough a minute to work between additions.

A hardball is rattling around in the bread pan: A serious lack of liquid, which means that you probably drank the beer that was supposed to be added. This is a great way to stress out your machine and shorten its life. Solution: Pull the ball, chisel it into smaller pieces, and throw it back in with more liquid. If it takes a while to get the dough into shape, you may want to stop the machine and restart it, to insure proper kneading.

No dough, mostly dry flour with a few wet globs: You did remember the liquid? Of course you did. It's obviously a bad recipe. Solution: Add liquid, and you might as well start with one-quarter cup. Watch and add as necessary.

Side-Stepping Delayed Starts

Machines that rest or heat up before getting to work can make the five-minute dough check into a thirty-minute dough check. If you want to cut down that time, you can generally short-circuit the process by using the dough cycle. This should start the machine immediately, and you can then listen, look, and poke until the dough is correct. Then just turn off the machine and restart it after picking the desired setting. (If you take this short-cut, be sure to have all ingredients at room temperature. One reason for the rest period is to insure that all ingredients are at the proper temperature. If they're not, you could wipe out the yeast.)

Likewise with timer settings: You can always start the machine, on the dough setting if necessary, to check and repair the dough, then turn it off, set the timer, and start it again. Since I don't like to let bread sit in the machine after baking, I often use this method to make sure that someone will be around when the bread is done. I also recommend this procedure when trying a new recipe, or with one that rises a lot; coming home to a dough that rose too high and burned is almost as much fun as a prostate examination, and is well worth a few minute's time to avoid.

Secrets for Making Great Bread

There is no reason why you cannot turn out consistently great bread from your machine. The following tips and recommendations are my "secrets" for making bread you can brag about.

- Start with fresh ingredients, especially yeast and flour.
- When baking with white flour, use only high-gluten bread flour. All-purpose flour will not produce loaves you can brag about.
- If your tap water is treated, and most is, buy bottled water to use in your machine. Using treated water almost guarantees mediocre results.
- Measure all ingredients accurately, especially those that affect the liquid-to-flour ratio.
- Always measure the same way, using the same tools.
- Baby-sit your machine for the first five to ten minutes for every loaf, if possible. This is the only way to overcome variables such as temperature, humidity, and the like.
- Don't let the loaf sit in the machine after baking or it will get disgustingly soggy.

As soon as you become familiar with the basics, you'll start turning out great bread on a regular basis. Even new recipes will turn out well. Eventually, you'll start making up your own recipes, although some of your creations will surely have family and friends questioning your sanity. Don't worry, it's simply a case of bread machine addiction. Is this a great machine or what?

CHAPTER 5

Bread and Dough Miscellany

Winging It

All bread machine chefs eventually wind up creating their own recipes. This is the fun part, and after you've learned a few basics, writing a new recipe is relatively easy. It's also tremendously satisfying to come up with a great new bread.

The guidelines below will give you a framework for your ideas; it is up to you to do the finishing work that will result in a delicious, personal creation. You can use the same guidelines to convert handmade recipes to bread machine recipes.

Here are the approximate ingredient quantities for a one-pound loaf:

²/₃ to 1 cup liquid
2 to 2¹/₂ cups flour
1 teaspoon to 2 tablespoons sugar/sweetener
¹/₂ to 1 teaspoon salt
1 teaspoon to 2 tablespoons fat
1¹/₂ to 2¹/₂ teaspoons yeast

Here are the approximate ingredients for a one-and-a-half-pound loaf:

1 to 1¼ cups liquid
3 to 4 cups flour
1 to 3 tablespoons sugar/sweetener
½ to 1½ teaspoons salt
1 to 3 tablespoons fat
2 to 3 teaspoons yeast

Notes About Ingredients

Liquid: The amount of liquid used depends on the amount and type of flour(s) used, and what other ingredients might be added. Whole grain breads use more flour than white breads to produce the same size loaf, which means that extra liquid must also be added.

Because they tend to absorb liquid slower than white bread doughs, doughs containing a high percentage of whole grain flour can appear to be too moist in the early stages. Resist the temptation to add extra flour in an attempt to make the dough less sticky.

If you add eggs, fruit, or vegetables, remember that all of these will add liquid to the dough, and therefore the amount of liquid should be reduced. Obviously, the use of honey as sweetener also requires a reduction in liquid.

Flour: The capacity of your machine determines the quantity of flour used, but it also depends on the kinds of flours to be added. If you are using only bread flour, do not exceed two cups in a one-pound machine, or three cups in a one-and-a-half-pounder. However, since whole wheat flour, rye flour, and other non-gluten flours do not rise as much as bread flour, combinations of flour can surpass those limits.

Don't go overboard and add two cups of whole wheat to two cups of bread flour in a one-pound machine; instead try one-and-a-half cups of bread flour and one cup of whole wheat. It always works best to replace some of the bread flour with the other flour(s), making the replacement amount larger than the amount reduced. Remember that the more bread flour used, the taller and lighter the resulting loaf.

If your first attempt is too short and dense, try again using more bread flour and less "other flour." A couple of trials should get you to the right size, texture, and flavor, although I will admit that I have occasionally had an embarrassing number of rejects before finally nailing down a good recipe.

Sugar/Sweetener: Too much sugar can cause yeast to self-destruct, and can result in an overly brown or burned crust. If you are adding other sweet ingredients to your dough, such as fruit, be aware that they contain sugar. In that case you might want to cut the sugar in half; or, in the case of super-sweet ingredients, perhaps even eliminate sugar from the recipe.

Salt: Because it adds to your bread in a number of ways, salt is a required ingredient. However, since one of its main functions is to inhibit yeast action, too much salt will halt yeast activity, resulting in a really short loaf. As with sugar, be aware that other ingredients, such as olives or cheese or salted nuts, can contain significant amounts of salt that must be taken into consideration.

Fat: Too much fat will shorten the gluten strands, leaving you with a short little heavyweight rather than a tall, proud, lightweight. Solid and liquid fats can be used interchangeably; and since they all end up in a liquid state, no adjustment is necessary to the liquid in the recipe. And again, be aware of other ingredients heavy in fat, such as cheese or sour cream. For instance, a loaf using sour cream as a liquid needs no additional fat.

Yeast: Sticking close to the recommended amounts of one-and-a-half teaspoons for a one-pound loaf, and two teaspoons for a one-and-a-half-pounder seems to produce the best results. An extra half-teaspoon to one teaspoon of yeast won't hurt, and can help really heavy breads, or breads with a lot of added ingredients; but doubling or tripling the amount will guarantee a failure. It's important that the dough rise just the right amount during the rising cycles, and too much yeast can throw that timing off.

Although it helps to stick reasonably close to the guidelines listed above, the liquid and flour amounts are the ones that really count. The main reason breads fail is that the liquid-to-flour ratio is off. Therefore be as accurate as possible with those two; a bit more or less of any of the other ingredients won't make all that much of a difference.

Above all, you've got to baby-sit all new creations. Since you're breaking new ground, just about anything can happen. So be prepared to spend the first ten minutes or so with your nose to your machine. That way, you can make any necessary repairs and at least give yourself a shot at a great loaf. While your repairs won't always give you a 100 percent batting average, at least you can insure that you'll wind up with a loaf that you can learn from. And as you continue to experiment and gain experience, you'll find yourself turning out more and more great breads on the very first try!

The Perfect Loaf

Okay, now that you've taken the time and trouble to learn how to make bread in your machine, how do you know if you've baked a great loaf? Tasting it is probably the best way to judge, but there are also other standards. Professional bakers look at the following to judge a loaf:

The shape should be more or less symmetrical, and the loaf should stand up proudly. A great loaf has an attitude and is proud to show it.

The crust should be neither pale nor blackened, but richly colored all over. It should also be at least somewhat crispy compared to the interior of the loaf.

The density and pattern of air cells or holes in a slice of bread should be even throughout the slice. And except for certain breads, the holes should be small and all about the same size.

The inside of a great loaf should feel soft, dry, and smooth. If you pull a piece from the loaf, it should tear off, rather than crumble. The inside of a great loaf will spring back after being briefly poked with a finger, rather than leave an indentation.

These standards do not apply to every loaf of bread. But they do give you a chance to look critically at the majority of the bread that you bake, and evaluate it as a professional baker would.

Miscellaneous Tips

If you're thinking there's no end to all this information about bread making, you're right! Here are a few more tips that I haven't covered elsewhere.

Dough Handling

If a recipe calls for a lightly floured work surface, use one or two tablespoons of flour. Spread it out with your hand before plopping down the dough, and also wipe some on the rolling pin if you're going to be rolling out the dough. When a recipe refers to a greased bowl, use a couple of teaspoons of oil or shortening to give the bowl a good coating. Or you can also use one of the vegetable type sprays for convenience.

When rising bread outside the bread machine, cover the dough with plastic wrap or waxed paper rather than a towel. Dough that rises up into a towel will stick to the towel and harden up like quick-drying cement.

Refrigerating Dough

You can refrigerate dough overnight for convenience or to make it easier to work with. (Chilling the dough makes it less elastic or rubbery, and it becomes easier to shape or roll out.) Simply punch down the dough after the first rising, cover with plastic wrap (removing as much air as possible), and refrigerate. To use, allow it to reach room temperature (at least two hours), shape, and set aside for the final rise before baking.

Cooling and Cutting Fresh Bread

Despite the fact that it is almost impossible to refrain from cutting into a warm loaf straight from the oven, there are good reasons to practice restraint, at least for the first few minutes. Freshly baked bread is full of moisture, and the starches in the bread are soggy rather than solid. Allowing the bread to sit for a few minutes gives the excess moisture a chance to steam away and allows the starches to grow a backbone and firm up the loaf.

You should always cut fresh bread with a real bread knife, one with circular serrations. Don't even think about using your big Buck knife; remember, always use the right tool for the job! If you need to buy a bread knife, look for one with the smallest serrations possible. The small serrations make slicing easier, and allow you to slice quite hot bread without tearing it to shreds.

When slicing, let the serrations and a back-and-forth motion do the cutting. Any downward pressure will tear and mash the bread rather than cut off nice, even slices.

Storing Bread

Since homemade bread is not loaded with preservatives and un-pronounceable, sixteen-syllable, laboratory chemicals, it's going to go stale quickly. The best way to store bread and keep it close to its original character is to use a bread box. I mean a real bread box, one designed to store bread. They work.

Second best is a paper bag with the mouth closed tight after each use. My next favorite is in a microwave oven. However, since it is almost a closed system, the microwave will hold in most of the moisture, which will rob the bread of every bit of crispness it was born with. Plastic bags are the same; they prevent the bread from drying out, but after a few hours, every loaf turns soft and moist. Which also makes an excellent breeding ground for a colorful assortment of molds.

Although storing bread in the frig tends to dry it out quickly, I have found that a couple of days in a frig, sealed in a plastic bag, can extend the edible life of a loaf. For longer storage, bread can be tightly wrapped in freezer paper and frozen. To thaw, set out at room temperature with the wrapping partially opened to allow excess moisture to evaporate.

High Altitude Adjustment

Altitudes above 3,000 feet can have a dramatic effect on your bread. At higher altitudes, the lower air pressure allows the loaf to rise so high that when the baking cycle begins, it collapses because the dough has stretched itself so thin that it can't support itself. The solution is rather obvious: Yeast activity must be slowed down, restricted, or reduced.

One effective method is to reduce the amount of yeast. Depending on the altitude, cut the yeast by one-quarter to one-half teaspoon. Since salt helps to restrict yeast activity, an increase of one-quarter to one-half teaspoon of salt will also help control the dough. Finally, since a stiff dough rises slower than a soft one, reducing the liquid will limit the ability of the dough to rise. I find it easier to play with the liquid than the yeast or salt. Since I baby-sit virtually every loaf, I just make sure that the bouncing ball of dough is drier when I'm up high, and a bit damper when I'm at sea level.

CHAPTER 6

Trouble-Shooting

*N*ot every loaf you make is going to be a contest winner, unless you're able to enter some of your spectacular failures in a "Bread from Hell" contest. Win some, lose some, no big deal. Failed loaves are simply learning experiences; the important thing is to figure out what went wrong so that you can correct it.

To begin with, are you sure you have a problem? Not every loaf will rise to the top of the pan and come out light and almost fluffy. Don't automatically conclude that all short, or dense loaves are failures. Has anyone ever seen a richly flavored, hearty dark rye bread that was as big as a loaf of white bread? Nope. But that doesn't mean that the rye has a problem. So before you look for a solution, first make sure you've got a problem.

Nearly all failed loaves are due to an incorrect liquid-to-flour ratio. Quite simply, the dough was either too wet or too dry. Sounds easy to fix, and most of the time it is. The problem is that the correct ratio is not only an unknown, it varies from day to day, as explained earlier. To repeat myself once again, the best solution is to keep an eye on the dough for the first five or ten

·minutes of mixing/kneading, and to make repairs at that time. This usually will solve any problems. However, when you do come up with a less than perfect loaf, the questions and answers below should provide a solution.

Uneven top, knotty, possibly even creases along sides where dough didn't fill pan?

The dough was too dry. Add more liquid on the next attempt. When you check the kneading dough, be sure that it is soft and elastic, rather than stiff and hard.

Mushroom-shaped loaves?

If the loaf is shaped like a healthy mushroom—that is, with a full, rounded top that curves down to the edge of the pan—and the bread otherwise looks and tastes okay, you've either pushed your machine a bit past its capacity or else used some really active yeast. Not a problem unless it's sticking to the top or sides of the machine. If it is sticking anywhere, double check that the recipe quantity is suitable for your machine, and cut it back if necessary. If the quantity is okay, try using a bit less liquid or a hair less yeast (reduce the amount by 1/4 teaspoon), or reduce the amount of sugar or sweetener.

If your loaf is mushroom shaped with a flat top that stretches across the pan (or even sinks down below the top of the pan), then your bread has risen too much and has collapsed. Make sure that you have used the correct setting for the bread that you are making, since some cycles allow extra rising time for denser breads. Reducing the liquid should solve the problem, as will cutting back on the yeast or sugar.

Sunken or soggy loaves?

Too much liquid. Don't forget that vegetables and fruits will add moisture and affect the outcome. Also make sure that you actually measure the liquid that you add to the recipe, rather than guesstimate. (For instance, my coffee cup looks like it should hold about a cup, but full to the brim it holds nearly one and three-quarters cups.)

Pale-colored loaves?

First make sure that the crust setting on your machine is not set to light. If you want a nice dark crust, set your machine on the middle setting or higher; and since sugar/sweetener is what gives the bread a dark crust, increase it slightly. Remember that extra sugar/sweetener will cause the yeast to work overtime, so if you increase it more than a teaspoon, add an extra pinch or two of salt to keep the yeast in line.

The smoke alarm is screaming and the loaf is hard to see because of the smoke!

Too much of everything. Once in a while, hopefully not more than once a lifetime for each of us—due to the position of the stars, the current NFL standings, or possibly even distracted stupidity—a loaf just goes berserk. If you've got more money than time, toss the machine and destroy the recipe. If you've got neither money nor time, like most of us, toss the recipe and try to find four hours or so to clean up the machine.

Here's what happened: The dough rose so much that it hit the top and sides of the machine before collapsing over the sides of the pan and falling on the heating element. Then, when the element turned on, the fun started. It's a hell of a mess that tests just how much you like your machine, and maybe even how much your mate likes both you and your machine. This is an experience that, along with passing a kidney stone, you never want to experience, so find out your machine's capacity, and try to come reasonably close when measuring ingredients.

Outside of loaf is soggy?

When the bake cycle ends, the bread will be steaming. If it continues to sit in the pan, the steam will condense on the pan and inside the baking chamber. So your bread takes a sauna bath, which essentially predigests the outer layer of the loaf. Great if you're under a year old or over ninety-nine and toothless, but miserable for the rest of us. The best idea is to get the bread out of the machine as soon as it has finished baking.

Short, squatty, dense loaves?

First, did you use the correct setting? Whole wheat loaves don't do well on a white bread setting.

What kind of flour did you use? If the flour was too low in gluten, your bread didn't have a chance. (See chapter 3, "Ingredients," for hints.)

Did you add enough (or any) yeast? You might also check to see how old your yeast is; improper storage and old age will turn your yeast into a real bad actor.

A lack of sugar can also contribute to this problem. Try adding more, a teaspoon at time.

If the dough is not moist enough, it can't rise. You might try adding more liquid. An excess of salt will also restrict yeast activity, so double check the recipe and make sure that only a minimum amount is added.

Finally, are you sure that the loaf wasn't supposed to be like that? Some of the darker whole grain breads never do grow up to be tall and handsome. Treasure them for their taste, not their looks. So if your bread knife will cut it, try a piece before you toss it.

The bread is hard to get out of the pan and/or the mixing paddle comes off in the bread?

Happens to me all the time. Fact is, some loaves never want to leave the womb, and on occasion the mixing paddle tries to escape by hiding in the bread. I make it a point to turn over every loaf when I remove it from the pan to see if the paddle has come off with the loaf. Otherwise, you won't realize it until you either try to cut the paddle in half with your bread knife (doing wonders for both paddle and knife!) or go to make another loaf, only to realize that the paddle is gone. Keep track of that paddle; without it, your machine is useless.

Dry, crumbly loaves?

These are usually due to too little moisture or fat. Authentic French bread is made without fat and is a good example of a dry loaf that produces lots of crumbs when sliced. To remedy that, simply add more oil or margarine to the dough.

Center of loaf not baked?

This problem generally arises with recipes that call for moist ingredients, such as bananas or applesauce, or ingredients such as bran or other whole grain flours. These recipes produce heavier doughs that easily become too wet and then bake unevenly. It really is important to keep an eye on these doughs, adding flour if necessary, to keep them moist rather than soggy.

CHAPTER 7

Other Helpful Tools

As good as bread machines are, they can't do it all. I have a number of other tools that I use along with the machine that help me turn out excellent breads.

Small rubber scraper: One tool that I use every time I make bread is a small rubber scraper that measures about one inch wide and two-and-a-half inches long. I've cut the handle down to about six inches in length, making it perfect for scraping down the sides of the bread pan after adding additional liquid or flour. Since it's small enough to avoid the mixing paddle, I can use it while the machine is running and frequently use it, rather than my finger, to poke my dough. It's also perfect for cleaning molasses or honey off measuring spoons, or sourdough starter from measuring cups.

Parchment paper: Parchment paper is heat-resistant paper that can be used to line baking sheets and pans. It will not burn at temperatures under 450 degrees. It eliminates the need to grease pans or sheets and so really cuts back on cleanup.

Cooling racks: These may seem unnecessary, but cooling breads do need to be kept off counters or flat surfaces. Freshly baked bread is steaming, and if that steam can't escape, it'll turn to water. Care to guess which will absorb that water, the bread or the countertop? Get a cooling rack or two. They'll save you from soggy bread, and they're cheap and easy to store.

Measuring spoons: These provide accurate measurements, which allow successful repeat performances. I prefer the circular stainless steel ones, but any are better than your stainless tableware. Two sets, one for wet ingredients and one for dry, keep things simple.

Electronic timer: I have really come to depend on a small electronic timer while I'm baking. Breads such as bagels or flatbreads always need timing while resting, rising, boiling, cooking, or baking, and the timer keeps my easily distracted mind from wandering too far. I especially like the repeat function when I'm doing repetitive actions like boiling bagels. This feature allows me to push stop when the buzzer goes off, and then without re-setting anything, just press start again as soon as a new batch of bagels hits the boiling water.

Dough scraper: This is nothing more than a large flat piece of metal with a handle along one edge, but it's a handy tool to have when dealing with dough. It can handle sticky doughs better than your hands and it's simpler to clean. A scraper will also cut dough into pieces a whole lot easier and faster than a knife.

PART II

Bread Machine Recipes

CHAPTER 8

White, Egg, and Sourdough Loaves

White Bread Recipes

I like white bread. Homemade or bakery white bread, that is. I'd be the last person to defend packaged supermarket white bread, the kind that sticks to your gums when you eat it. That's not real bread. I'm talking about chewy loaves of French bread with hard, crisp crusts or tangy sourdough loaves. Can anyone truthfully say that they don't enjoy eating bread like that?

Basic White Bread

I like this loaf with a darker, crisper crust, so I generally bake it on the dark crust setting. Some machines, however, might tend to almost blacken the crust on this setting, so try a small loaf first to test out your machine.

1-POUND LOAF

²/₃ cup water
1 tablespoon margarine
2 cups bread flour
1 tablespoon sugar

¾ teaspoon salt
1 ½ tablespoons dry milk
   powder
1 ½ teaspoons yeast

1½-POUND LOAF

1 cup + 1 tablespoon water
1 tablespoon margarine
3 cups bread flour
4 teaspoons sugar

1 teaspoon salt
2 tablespoons dry milk powder
2 teaspoons yeast

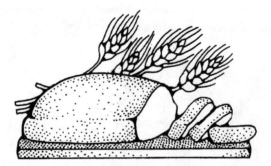

Two-Day White Bread

This recipe is an example of a bread made from a sponge, a method that can be used for most bread recipes. To a baker, a sponge is a mixture of yeast, liquid, and flour that is allowed to ferment until light and spongy. Typically, sponges are made from a portion of the ingredients in a recipe, and the balance of ingredients are added after a period of fermentation. Using a sponge gives the gluten a chance to develop and provides the bread with greater flavor and a finer texture.

So in order to give this loaf a bit more flavor and height, it gets "started" the night before. No real extra work, but a better loaf. If you want to try using the sponge method with other bread recipes, simply use the same quantities listed under "Starter," below, substituting liquids or flours according to the recipe you're following. You should notice a difference in the flavor, texture, and possibly even the height of your bread.

1-POUND LOAF

Starter*:
1/2 cup water
1 cup bread flour
1/2 teaspoon yeast

Additional Ingredients**:
1/4 cup water
1 tablespoon margarine
1 cup bread flour
2 teaspoons sugar
3/4 teaspoon salt
1 teaspoon yeast

1 1/2-POUND LOAF

Starter*:
1/2 cup water
1 cup bread flour
1/2 teaspoon yeast

Additional Ingredients**:
1/2 cup + 1 tablespoon water
1 tablespoon margarine
2 cups bread flour
1 tablespoon sugar
1 teaspoon salt
1 teaspoon yeast

*Put the starter ingredients in the machine the night before and mix well for five minutes on the dough setting before turning the machine off. Close the lid and let sit until the next day, when it will be bubbly and slightly "ripe."

**Add these ingredients the following day and start the machine as usual. It always pays to keep an eye on the dough for the first five minutes or so, just in case repairs are necessary.

French Bread

Be sure to select the French or European setting. This will give the bread plenty of time to rise, and a nice crisp, crunchy crust. Plan on eating it quickly—with no fat and just a little sugar, it will turn stale within a day or two.

1-POUND LOAF

3/4 cup + 1 tablespoon water   1/2 teaspoon salt
2 1/4 cups bread flour   1 1/2 teaspoons yeast
1 teaspoon sugar

1 1/2-POUND LOAF

1 cup + 3 tablespoons water   1/2 teaspoon salt
3 1/2 cups bread flour   2 teaspoons yeast
2 teaspoons sugar

Sweet Butter Bread

This one's a crowd pleaser, tall, golden, and delicious. If the crust turns out too dark, use the light setting.

1-POUND LOAF

1/4 cup water   2 1/4 cups bread flour
1/3 cup milk   2 tablespoons sugar
1 large egg   1 teaspoon salt
3 tablespoons butter   1 1/2 teaspoons yeast

1 1/2-POUND LOAF

1/2 cup water   3 1/4 cups bread flour
1/2 cup milk   3 tablespoons sugar
1 large egg   1 1/2 teaspoons salt
5 tablespoons butter   2 teaspoons yeast

Buttermilk Bread

Made with cultured buttermilk, this tangy, tight-textured bread has an old-fashioned flavor.

1-POUND LOAF

3/4 cup buttermilk
1 teaspoon vinegar
2 tablespoons margarine
2 1/4 cups bread flour

2 teaspons sugar
3/4 teaspoon salt
1 1/2 teaspoons yeast

1 1/2-POUND LOAF

1 cup + 2 tablespoons
   buttermilk
1 1/2 teaspoons vinegar
3 tablespoons margarine

3 1/4 cups bread flour
1 tablespoon sugar
1 teaspoon salt
1 teaspoon yeast

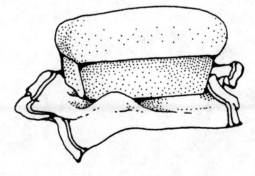

Pepperoni Bread

A white loaf with a pepperoni taste. Makes great cheese sandwiches.

1-POUND LOAF

3/4 cup water
1 tablespoon margarine
2 cups bread flour
4 teaspoons sugar
1 teaspoon salt
1 tablespoon dry milk
    powder
1 1/2 teaspoons yeast

Add at Beep:
1/2 cup (about 2 ounces) sliced
    pepperoni, slices halved into
    semicircles
1 tablespoon bread flour

1 1/2-POUND LOAF

1 cup water
1 1/2 tablespoons margarine
3 cups bread flour
2 tablespoons sugar
1 1/2 teaspoons salt
2 tablespoons dry milk
    powder
2 teaspoons yeast

Add at Beep:
3/4 cup (about 3 ounces) sliced
    pepperoni, slices halved into
    semicircles
1 1/2 tablespoons bread flour

Sour Cream Bread

This picture-perfect loaf is not only tall and light, but wonderfully tasty. You'll make this one more than once.

1-POUND LOAF

1/4 cup water
2/3 cup sour cream
2 cups bread flour
1 1/2 teaspoons sugar

3/4 teaspoon salt
2 tablespoons dry milk powder
1 1/2 teaspoons yeast

1 1/2-POUND LOAF

1/2 cup + 1 tablespoon water
3/4 cup sour cream
3 cups bread flour
2 teaspoons sugar

1 teaspoon salt
3 tablespoons dry milk powder
2 teaspoons yeast

Sour Cream Poppy Seed Bread

A delicious, light, tall loaf with a fine texture.

1-POUND LOAF

1/4 cup water
1/3 cup sour cream
1 large egg
1 tablespoon margarine
2 cups bread flour

1 tablespoon sugar
3/4 teaspoon salt
1 1/2 teaspoons poppy seeds
1 1/2 teaspoons yeast

1 1/2-POUND LOAF

1/3 cup water
1/2 cup sour cream
1 large egg
2 tablespoons margarine
3 cups bread flour

1 1/2 tablespoons sugar
1 teaspoon salt
2 teaspoons poppy seeds
2 teaspoons yeast

Egg Bread Recipes

When mixing a dough that includes eggs, it's important to keep an eye on the dough in the early stages. Even if you use USDA large eggs (and you should), egg size can vary, and this can throw off the liquid-to-flour ratio enough to ruin your loaf. So just baby-sit and repair as needed.

Egg Bread

Everyone loves this good-looking, tasty loaf.

1-POUND LOAF

2 large eggs + water to make
  3/4 cup liquid
1 tablespoon margarine
2 1/4 cups bread flour

1 tablespoon sugar
1 teaspoon salt
2 tablespoons dry milk powder
1 1/2 teaspoons yeast

1 1/2-POUND LOAF

3 large eggs + water to make
  1 cup + 2 tablespoons
  liquid
1 1/2 tablespoons margarine
3 1/4 cups bread flour

1 1/2 tablespoons sugar
1 1/2 teaspoons salt
3 tablespoons dry milk powder
2 teaspoons yeast

Bacon Egg Bread

A great-looking loaf with a distinct bacon flavor. Have it toasted for breakfast along with your (what else?) bacon and eggs.

1-POUND LOAF

2 large eggs + water to make
  ³/₄ cup liquid
1 tablespoon margarine
2 cups bread flour

2 teaspoons sugar
1 teaspoon salt
4 slices bacon,* cooked crisp
1 ¹/₂ teaspoons yeast

1 ¹/₂-POUND LOAF

3 large eggs + water to make
  1 cup + 2 tablespoons
  liquid
1 ¹/₂ tablespoons margarine
3 cups bread flour

1 tablespoon sugar
1 ¹/₂ teaspoons salt
6 slices bacon,* cooked crisp
2 teaspoons yeast

*No need to crumble up the bacon; simply break each slice into a couple of pieces and add to the pan. The machine will do the work.

Egg Muffin Bread

This golden-colored bread is rich and delicious. Be sure to try it toasted.

1-POUND LOAF

2 large eggs + water to make
    $^2/_3$ cup
2 tablespoons margarine
2 $^1/_4$ cups bread flour

1 tablespoon sugar
1 teaspoon salt
3 tablespoons dry milk powder
1 $^1/_2$ teaspoons yeast

1 $^1/_2$-POUND LOAF

3 large eggs + water to make
    1 cup
3 tablespoons margarine
3 $^1/_4$ cups bread flour

1 $^1/_2$ tablespoons sugar
1 $^1/_2$ teaspoons salt
4 tablespoons dry milk powder
2 teaspoons yeast

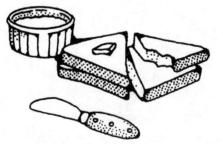

Sourdough Bread Recipes

It's amusing and somewhat reassuring these days when every-thing is networked and "online," that something as old and nontechnical as a slightly spoiled dough can produce such a deli-cious and popular bread.

Sourdough bread is made from a prepared starter composed of yeast, flour, and a liquid. The distinctive sour flavor varies ac-cording to the particular yeast involved. Every area has its own unique strains, some more tasty than others. San Francisco clearly has a healthy climate for some fine-tasting yeasts.

Good starters can be made, purchased, or borrowed. If you're lucky, perhaps a fellow bread maker will share some with you. Once you have a starter, it's a simple matter to keep and maintain it indefinitely—some starters have been handed down for generations—as well as increase it so that you too can give some away. One word of warning: Unlike active dry yeast, which can sit unused and lonely in your frig for months at a time, sourdough starter does require periodic maintenance. If you love sourdough, however, the small amount of time and labor in-volved is loose change, gladly spent.

If you'd like to try growing your own, try one of the follow-ing recipes, either Airborne Starter or Grape Starter. A word of caution: I have tried the Airborne Starter recipe any number of times, and have yet to come up with an active mixture. I'm beginning to think that the super dry, high desert climate here in Albuquerque is too harsh for the necessary airborne molds. Wild yeasts, however, are another matter. Found on organic material, they are responsible for the light white film found on the skin of shiny fruits such as grapes and plums. In contrast to my failures with airborne molds, I have made some excellent sourdough starters using grapes. If you too have trouble attracting molds, try the Grape Starter recipe.

Airborne Starter

Be sure to use bottled water for this recipe. Yeasts and molds do not do well in treated water, and your taste buds will also appreciate pure water.

1 cup untreated water
1 1/2 cups bread flour
1 teaspoon active dry yeast

1. Mix the ingredients together in a small bowl. Cover the mixture loosely and place in a warm location for 4 to 8 days, stirring once a day. It should bubble, and it may even bubble over the top. If that's the case, you've got a good, active starter. Stir in a little water and enough flour to make the consistency like a thin pancake batter.

2. If a liquid forms on top, just stir it back in. However, if the liquid turns color (other than just looking dark), say pink or purple, dump it and start over. Likewise to a foul-smelling starter; after all, sour is sour, but rotten is dead and out of here! Once your starter is the proper consistency and has taken on a distinctive sour smell, it is ready to use. Cover and refrigerate.

Grape Starter

When shopping for grapes for this recipe, look for those with the heaviest "film" on them. Since you will not wash the grapes before using, organic grapes are preferred.

1 cup bread flour
1 1/2 cups untreated water
1/2 pound organic grapes, unwashed

1. Mix up the flour and water in a good-sized bowl, push the grapes under the surface, cover loosely, and set in a warm spot.

2. Come back the next day and mix it up as well as possible, adding a couple tablespoons each of flour and water. By the second or third day, your starter should start to bubble. If, after stirring and feeding it for 4 days or so, all you've got is a lifeless pot of paste, toss it and try to find some grapes with a heavier film on them.

3. Once your starter is bubbling and expanding and smelling sweetly sour, pull out the grapes and pour the starter into a clean glass jar. It is now ready to use. Cover and refrigerate.

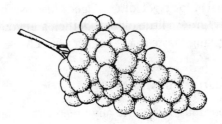

Using and Maintaining Your Starter

To use your homemade starter, measure out what you need for your bread. If it came straight from the frig, allow it to come to room temperature. You must then feed the starter jar an equal amount. If you pull out one cup of starter, add one cup each of flour and water and stir well. Let it sit at room temperature with a loose lid for a day, then cover and refrigerate it.

If a week or two go by without using your starter, it's time to refresh it. (This is the extra work I referred to above.) To do so simply pull out one cup of starter and feed as above, with one cup each of flour and water. Don't forget to leave it out at room temperature for a day. This will keep those hungry little wild yeast cells happy and alive for as long as you remember to take care of them. Starters that are literally hundreds of years old are not all that uncommon.

Long-Term Storage

If you're going to be gone, or otherwise know that you won't be able to feed your starter, you can freeze it. Transfer it to a plastic container that will allow for expansion, and toss into the freezer. To use, allow to warm up for a day, feed it, and allow it to sit for another day before using.

Sourdough Flavor

A good sourdough starter is like a good bottle of wine in that the flavor improves with age. Young starters often seem weak or one-dimensional. Don't get discouraged; just use or feed your starter regularly, grow a little older together, and your starter will develop a sour, tangy taste that'll pucker your cheeks.

Sourdough Starter Substitution

You can add sourdough starter to any bread recipe, although certain combinations work better than others. If you have starter available, experiment at will; after all, it's easy enough to make more starter! The only adjustment necessary is to the liquid in the recipe. When adding starter, count half the amount of starter as liquid and adjust the recipe accordingly. So using one cup of starter would add one-half cup of liquid, which you should then subtract from the liquid called for in that recipe.

Sourdough as Yeast

Although it is possible to make a loaf of sourdough bread without any added yeast, it takes a lot of extra time and trouble. What we're really after is flavor and convenience, so we just add extra yeast. The results are basically identical, except that adding yeast allows us to treat sourdough just like any other bread in our machines.

Sourdough Bread

A good sourdough starter together with this recipe will produce loaves that disappear quickly. Be prepared to make this often.

1-Pound Loaf

1/3 cup water	1 teaspoon sugar
3/4 cup sourdough starter	3/4 teaspoon salt
1 tablespoon margarine	1 1/2 teaspoons yeast
2 1/4 cups flour	

1 1/2-Pound Loaf

2/3 cup water	1 1/2 teaspoons sugar
1 cup sourdough starter	1 teaspoon salt
1 1/2 tablespoons margarine	2 teaspoons yeast
3 1/2 cups flour	

Sourdough French Bread

Hard to beat this bread, in my book. This is the kind of bread that makes me a strong defender of white bread! Be sure to use the French or European setting.

1-Pound Loaf

1/4 cup water	1/2 teaspoon sugar
3/4 cup sourdough starter	1/2 teaspoon salt
2 cups bread flour	1 1/2 teaspoons yeast

1 1/2-Pound Loaf

1/2 cup water	3/4 teaspoon sugar
1 cup sourdough starter	3/4 teaspoon salt
3 cups bread flour	2 teaspoons yeast

English Sourdough

Add the baking soda directly to the water in the bread pan, mix it in, and allow it to sit for a minute before adding the other ingredients. As soon as the starter is added, the mixture gets real active! This produces a finely textured, tasty sourdough bread.

1-POUND LOAF

¹/₃ cup water
¹/₂ teaspoon baking soda
²/₃ cup sourdough starter
2 teaspoons canola oil
2 teaspoons honey

2 cups bread flour
³/₄ teaspoon salt
2 tablespoons dry milk
   powder
1 ¹/₂ teaspoons yeast

1 ¹/₂-POUND LOAF

¹/₂ cup water
¹/₂ teaspoon baking soda
1 cup sourdough starter
1 tablespoon canola oil
1 tablespoon honey

3 cups bread flour
1 teaspoon salt
3 tablespoons dry milk
   powder
2 teaspoons yeast

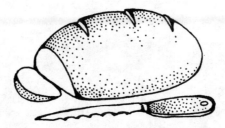

Mount Olympus Sourdough

Hardly an accompaniment, this strongly-flavored, hearty bread is more like an entrée. Since this is a short loaf, no one-pound recipe is necessary. The sun-dried tomatoes used in this recipe are the dry packaged ones, not the ones preserved in oil.

1 1/2-POUND LOAF

1/4 cup water
1 cup sourdough starter
2 tablespoons olive oil
3 cups bread flour
1 tablespoon sugar
1/4 teaspoon salt
3 ounces feta cheese, crumbled
3/4 teaspoon garlic powder

2 tablespoons chopped sun-dried tomatoes*
1 teaspoon oregano
2 teaspoons yeast

Add at Beep:
10 Greek olives, pitted and quartered

*Sun-dried tomatoes can be difficult to chop with a knife. Just snip them into strips with a scissors.

CHAPTER 9

Whole Wheat, Rye, and Other Hearty Loaves

*H*ere are the breads that we can really sink our teeth into, chewy breads with body and bold flavors. Unfortunately, these breads tend to be more of a challenge to bread machine chefs, mainly because of the lower gluten content of whole wheat and rye flour. Less gluten means smaller loaves. In addition, whole wheat flour includes bran, which is heavy compared to the rest of the flour. This also makes it hard for the dough to rise very high. In general, 100 percent whole wheat and rye breads are height-challenged. There are, however, steps that we can take to help them stand tall.

One of the most effective remedies is to double-knead the dough. After the machine has finished the initial mixing and kneading cycle, hit the stop button to turn it off, and then just restart it. This accomplishes two things. First, it allows extra time for whole wheat and rye flour to absorb water. Both tend to absorb slowly, which is why many machines rest before starting whole wheat cycles. If your machine is one that rests first, you can generally get the ball rolling immediately by starting the machine on the dough cycle. When the kneading ends, simply stop the machine, and start again on a whole wheat cycle.

The other benefit from double-kneading is that the little amount of gluten present has more of a chance to develop, which will lead to a taller loaf. Virtually all breads will benefit from double-kneading, although the results will certainly be more evident in wheat and rye loaves. The only drawback is the extra time involved, as well as the fact that someone has to hang around to restart the machine.

The other weapon that we have against short-statured loaves is vital gluten. Since whole wheat and rye flour are both low in gluten, we can simply add more gluten to our recipes. Typically, one tablespoon of vital gluten (75 percent protein) per cup of flour will do the trick.

In the end, the fact remains that breads made from whole grain flours just do not rise as much as those made from bread flour. So although there are a number of things that we can do to help these little loaves, we simply have to settle for some shorter loaves, and perhaps even a gnarly or slightly fallen top. The only possible problem is an aesthetic one, since the spectacular flavor of these loaves will be unaffected.

One final thing to remember about "heavy" breads. Whole wheat flours not only absorb liquid slowly, they also tend to absorb more liquid. So be prepared to add additional liquid to your recipes. In fact, since they soak up a lot of liquid as they rise, whole grain doughs should be tacky to sticky, rather than smooth to tacky.

Whole Wheat Bread

Use the whole wheat setting for this 100 percent whole wheat bread.

1-POUND LOAF

3/4 cup + 2 tablespoons water
3/4 tablespoon vegetable oil
3/4 tablespoon molasses
2 1/4 cups whole wheat flour

3/4 teaspoon salt
3 tablespoons vital gluten
2 teaspoons yeast

1 1/2-POUND LOAF

1 1/3 cups water
2 tablespoons vegetable oil
1 tablespoon molasses
3 1/2 cups whole wheat flour

1 teaspoon salt
4 tablespoons vital gluten
2 1/2 teaspoons yeast

Deter's Whole Wheat Bread

Developed by Francie Deter from Socorro, this recipe produces a tall and light loaf of wheat bread. And I do mean tall; try the one-pounder first, just to be safe!

1-POUND LOAF

1 cup water
1/4 cup canola oil
1/4 cup honey
1 cup + 1 tablespoon
    bread flour

1 1/2 cups whole wheat flour
1 teaspoon salt
1/4 cup dry milk powder
1/4 cup vital gluten
1 tablespoon yeast

1 1/2-POUND LOAF

1 1/2 cups water
1/3 cup canola oil
1/3 cup honey
1 1/2 cups bread flour
2 1/4 cups whole wheat flour

1 1/2 teaspoons salt
1/3 cup dry milk powder
1/3 cup vital gluten
1 1/2 tablespoons yeast

Cracked Wheat Bread

The cracked wheat used in this bread is literally the wheat berry cracked in half. It has not been boiled, and is not called bulgur. Great flavor and texture, another of my favorites.

1-POUND LOAF

3/4 cup water
2 tablespoons margarine
1 cup bread flour
2/3 cup whole wheat flour
1/3 cup cracked wheat

1 1/2 teaspoons sugar
1/2 teaspoon malt powder
1/2 teaspoon salt
2 tablespoons vital gluten
2 teaspoons yeast

1 1/2-POUND LOAF

1 1/4 cups water
2 tablespoons margarine
1 1/2 cups bread flour
1 cup whole wheat flour
1/2 cup cracked wheat

2 teaspoons sugar
1 teaspoon malt powder
1 teaspoon salt
3 tablespoons vital gluten
2 1/2 teaspoons yeast

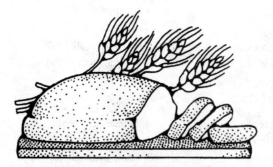

Cranberry Wheat Bread

The slightly bittersweet taste of the cranberries goes well with the flavor of the wheat to produce this great breakfast bread.

1-POUND LOAF

³/₄ cup water
2 tablespoons honey
2 tablespoons margarine
1 ¹/₂ cups bread flour
¹/₂ cup whole wheat flour

1 teaspoon salt
¹/₂ teaspoon ground nutmeg
¹/₂ cup dried cranberries*
1 ¹/₂ teaspoons yeast

1¹/₂-POUND LOAF

1 ¹/₄ cups water
3 tablespoons honey
3 tablespoons margarine
2 cups bread flour
1 cup whole wheat flour

1 ¹/₂ teaspoons salt
1 teaspoon ground nutmeg
³/₄ cup cranberries*
2 ¹/₂ teaspoons yeast

*I have found that the cranberries hold their own through the mixing and kneading cycles, and therefore it's unnecessary to wait for the beep before adding them.

The Ultimate Sandwich Bread

I haven't found anyone who doesn't like this bread, hence its name. The loaf is tall and light, which pleases even finicky eaters or children. The addition of both whole wheat and rye flours give the bread a rich, full flavor that satisfies those with more sophisticated tastes, yet the flavor is not so over-powering that it dominates sandwich fillings. One of my best loaves—a personal favorite.

1-POUND LOAF

²/₃ cup water
1 ½ tablespoons canola oil
1 cup bread flour
³/₄ cup whole wheat flour
¹/₄ cup rye flour

1 ½ tablespoons vital gluten
1 ½ tablespoons sugar
³/₄ teaspoon salt
1 ½ teaspoons yeast

1½-POUND LOAF

1 cup water
2 tablespoons canola oil
1³/₄ cups bread flour
1 cup whole wheat flour
¹/₃ cup rye flour

2 tablespoons vital gluten
2 tablespoons sugar
1 teaspoon salt
2 teaspoons yeast

7-Grain Bread

Made with a 7-grain cereal, this recipe works as well with 5-grain or 9-grain or whatever you can find locally. This healthy loaf is short but full flavored.

1-POUND LOAF

3/4 cup water
1 tablespoon margarine
1 1/4 cups bread flour
2/3 cup whole wheat flour

2 tablespoons sugar
1 teaspoon salt
3/4 cup 7-grain cereal
1 1/2 teaspoons yeast

1 1/2-POUND LOAF

1 cup + 2 tablespoons water
1 1/2 tablespoons margarine
2 2/3 cups bread flour
3/4 cup whole wheat flour

3 tablespoons sugar
1 1/2 teaspoons salt
1 cup 7-grain cereal
2 teaspoons yeast

Bran Bread

This healthy bread, while short with a close texture, is still quite light and tasty.

1-POUND LOAF

3/4 cup water
1 tablespoon margarine
2 cups bread flour
2 tablespoons sugar

1 teaspoon salt
1/2 cup wheat bran or oat bran
1 1/2 teaspoons yeast

1 1/2-POUND LOAF

1 cup + 2 tablespoons water
1 1/2 tablespoons margarine
3 cups bread flour
3 tablespoons sugar

1 1/2 teaspoons salt
3/4 cup wheat bran or oat bran
2 teaspoons yeast

Swedish Rye

A small, flavorful loaf with a hint of orange. A good sandwich bread.

1-POUND LOAF

3/4 cup water
1 tablespoon margarine
2 tablespoons honey
1 1/3 cups bread flour
2/3 cup rye flour

1 teaspoon salt
1 teaspoon caraway seeds
1 teaspoon dried orange peel,*
   soaked
1 1/2 teaspoons yeast

1 1/2-POUND LOAF

1 cup + 2 tablespoons water
1 1/2 tablespoons margarine
3 tablespoons honey
2 cups bread flour
1 cup rye flour

1 1/2 teaspoons salt
1 1/2 teaspoons caraway seeds
1 1/2 teaspoons dried orange
   peel,* soaked
2 teaspoons yeast

*Dried orange peel, unsoaked, has the consistency of hardwood. Soak it for at least thirty minutes, and be sure to drain it well before adding.

White Rye Bread

Short and lighter than a dark rye, but still very tasty.

1-POUND LOAF

³/₄ cup water
2 teaspoons margarine
1¹/₂ cups bread flour
¹/₂ cup rye flour
4 teaspoons sugar

1 teaspoon salt
2 tablespoons dry milk powder
1 teaspoon caraway seeds
1¹/₂ teaspoons yeast

1¹/₂-POUND LOAF

1 cup + 2 tablespoons water
3 teaspoons margarine
2¹/₄ cup bread flour
³/₄ cup rye flour
2 tablespoons sugar

1¹/₂ teaspoons salt
3 tablespoons dry milk powder
1¹/₂ teaspoons caraway seeds
2 teaspoons yeast

Onion Rye Bread

A bread that turns a sandwich from a snack into a meal.

1-POUND LOAF

³/₄ cup water
1 tablespoon margarine
2 cups bread flour
¹/₂ cup rye flour
4 teaspoons sugar

1 teaspoon salt
2 tablespoons dry milk powder
¹/₃ cup chopped onion
1 teaspoon caraway seeds
1¹/₂ teaspoons yeast

1¹/₂-POUND LOAF

1 cup + 2 tablespoons water
1¹/₂ tablespoons margarine
3 cups bread flour
³/₄ cup rye flour
2 tablespoons sugar

1¹/₂ teaspoons salt
3 tablespoons dry milk powder
¹/₂ cup chopped onion
1¹/₂ teaspoons caraway seeds
2 teaspoons yeast

Beer Rye Bread

Good height and good flavor make this a good bread. Use a whole wheat setting, with a light crust, if available. Make sure that the beer is flat and at room temperature. I generally measure it out the night before and leave it out until I make the bread.

1-POUND LOAF

2/3 cup flat beer
1 1/2 tablespoons canola oil
3/4 cup bread flour
1/2 cup whole wheat flour
1/3 cup rye flour
3/4 tablespoon packed brown
   sugar

1 teaspoon salt
1 1/2 tablespoons dry milk
   powder
1 1/2 tablespoons cornmeal
1 1/2 teaspoons caraway seeds
3/4 tablespoon dill weed
1 1/2 teaspoons yeast

1 1/2-POUND LOAF

1 cup flat beer
2 tablespoons canola oil
1 1/4 cups bread flour
2/3 cup whole wheat flour
1/2 cup rye flour
1 tablespoon packed brown
   sugar

1 1/2 teaspoons salt
2 tablespoons dry milk powder
2 tablespoons cornmeal
2 teaspoons caraway seeds
1 tablespoon dill weed
2 teaspoons yeast

Bitter Beer Rye

Good tangy flavor in this short loaf. Slice thin and enjoy this hearty bread. Make sure that the beer is flat and at room temperature. I generally measure it out the night before and leave it out until I make the bread.

1-POUND LOAF

½ cup flat beer
2 tablespoons cider vinegar
1 tablespoon margarine
1 cup bread flour
⅓ cup whole wheat flour
⅓ cup rye flour

1½ tablespoons packed
  brown sugar
1 teaspoon caraway seeds
1½ teaspoons dill weed
2 tablespoons vital gluten
2 teaspoons yeast

1½-POUND LOAF

¾ cup flat beer
3 tablespoons cider vinegar
1 tablespoon margarine
1½ cups bread flour
½ cup whole wheat flour
½ cup rye flour

2 tablespoons packed
  brown sugar
1½ teaspoons caraway seeds
2 teaspoons dill weed
3 tablespoons vital gluten
2½ teaspoons yeast

Light Sourdough Rye

Super flavor, excellent for sandwiches. Make sure that the beer is flat and at room temperature; I generally measure it out the night before and leave it out until I make the bread.

1-POUND LOAF

1/2 cup flat beer
1/2 cup sourdough starter
1 large egg
1 tablespoon margarine
1 1/2 cups + 2 tablespoons
  bread flour
1/2 cup rye flour
4 teaspoons sugar

1 teaspoon salt
3 tablespoons dry milk powder
1/4 cup cornmeal
1 1/2 teaspoons caraway seeds
1 tablespoon dried lemon peel,*
  soaked
1 1/2 teaspoons yeast

1 1/2-POUND LOAF

3/4 cup flat beer
3/4 cup sourdough starter
1 large egg
1 1/2 tablespoons margarine
2 1/4 cups bread flour
3/4 cup rye flour
2 tablespoons sugar

1 1/2 teaspoons salt
1/4 cup dry milk powder
1/3 cup cornmeal
2 teaspoons caraway seeds
1 1/2 tablespoons dried lemon
  peel,* soaked
2 teaspoons yeast

*Dried lemon peel, unsoaked, has the consistency of hardwood. Soak it for at least thirty minutes, and be sure to drain it well before adding.

Sourdough Rye

A compact little loaf with a load-and-a-half of flavor. This is a bread of substance.

1-POUND LOAF

1/2 cup water	2 1/2 cups bread flour
1 cup rye sourdough starter*	3/4 cup rye flour
1 large egg	2 teaspoons caraway seeds
2 tablespoons canola oil	2 teaspoons yeast
1 tablespoon molasses	

1 1/2-POUND LOAF

3/4 cup water	1 1/2 tablespoons molasses
1 1/2 cups rye sourdough starter*	3 1/2 cups bread flour
1 large egg	1 cup rye flour
3 tablespoons canola oil	2 teaspoons caraway seeds
	2 teaspoons yeast

*To make a rye starter, add one-half cup each water and rye flour to one cup of sourdough starter. For the following two days, pull out one-half cup of the starter and add another one-half cup of water and rye flour. By the fourth day, the starter should have taken on a very sharp smell, which means it is ready to use. Maintain the rye starter the same as a regular sourdough starter. If it gets too sharp or bitter, feed it once or twice with bread flour instead of rye.

Dark Russian Rye Bread

A short, dense, almost black loaf that's loaded with flavor. If some light breads are like cake, this bread is more like a steak.

1-POUND LOAF

3/4 cup water
1 tablespoon margarine
2 tablespoons molasses
3/4 cup bread flour
3/4 cup whole wheat flour

1/2 cup rye flour
3/4 teaspoon salt
2 teaspoons instant coffee
1/4 teaspoon crushed fennel seed
2 teaspoons yeast

1 1/2-POUND LOAF

1 1/4 cups water
2 tablespoons margarine
3 tablespoons molasses
1 1/4 cups bread flour
1 1/4 cups whole wheat flour

3/4 cup rye flour
1 1/4 teaspoons salt
1 tablespoon instant coffee
1/2 teaspoon crushed fennel seed
3 teaspoons yeast

Light Pumpernickel

A wonderful loaf, full of flavor with a solid body, but not overly heavy in either texture or flavor. Terrific sandwich bread.

1-POUND LOAF

³/₄ cup water
1 tablespoon canola oil
1 tablespoon molasses
1¹/₂ tablespoons honey
1 cup bread flour
²/₃ cup whole wheat flour

¹/₃ cup rye flour
³/₄ teaspoon salt
1¹/₂ tablespoons cocoa*
1¹/₂ teaspoons caraway seeds
1¹/₂ teaspoons yeast

1¹/₂-POUND LOAF

1 cup + 2 tablespoons water
1¹/₂ tablespoons canola oil
4 teaspoons molasses
2 tablespoons honey
1¹/₂ cups bread flour
1 cup whole wheat flour

¹/₂ cup rye flour
1 teaspoon salt
2 tablespoons cocoa*
2 teaspoons caraway seeds
2 teaspoons yeast

*Use only unsweetened or baking cocoa. (Sweetened cocoa is used for making drinking cocoa or hot chocolate.)

Pumpernickel Bread

Short, heavy, dense, and delicious, this dark, full-flavored loaf is unbeat-able when served with a hearty, thick soup or stew. (Double knead this recipe for sure!)

1-POUND LOAF

³/₄ cup water
2 tablespoons canola oil
2 tablespoons molasses
1 cup bread flour
¹/₂ cup whole wheat flour
¹/₂ cup rye flour

4 teaspoons sugar
1 teaspoon salt
1 tablespoon cocoa*
¹/₄ teaspoon instant coffee
1 teaspoon caraway seeds
2 teaspoons yeast

1¹/₂-POUND LOAF

1 cup + 2 tablespoons water
3 tablespoons canola oil
3 tablespoons molasses
1¹/₂ cups bread flour
³/₄ cup whole wheat flour
³/₄ cup rye flour

2 tablespoons sugar
1¹/₂ teaspoons salt
2 tablespoons cocoa*
¹/₂ teaspoon instant coffee
1¹/₂ teaspoons caraway seeds
3 teaspoons yeast

*Use only unsweetened or baking cocoa. (Sweetened cocoa is used for making drinking cocoa or hot chocolate.)

CHAPTER 10

Chile, Cheese, and Ethnic Loaves

*H*ot chile bread ahead—watch out, it may bite back! Also included are some delicious cheese breads. Don't be dismayed by a slightly sunken top on a cheese loaf; this is common.

Taco Cheddar Cheese Bread

A Southwestern flavor treat. Adjust the taco mix according to taste. (Four tea-spoons makes a strongly flavored loaf.)

1-POUND LOAF

3/4 cup water	1/2 teaspoon salt
2 teaspoons margarine	4 teaspoons dry taco mix
2 cups bread flour	2/3 cup grated cheddar cheese
2 teaspoons sugar	1 1/2 teaspoons yeast

1 1/2 -POUND LOAF

1 cup + 2 tablespoons water	3/4 teaspoon salt
1 tablespoon margarine	2 tablespoons dry taco mix
3 cups bread flour	1 cup grated cheddar cheese
1 tablespoon sugar	2 teaspoons yeast

Jalapeño Cheese Bread

Vary the heat by changing the quantity of jalapeño added. This recipe has a good "bite" and is rated hot.

1-POUND LOAF

2/3 cup water	2 tablespoons seeded and
2 cups bread flour	chopped jalapeño chile
1 tablespoon sugar	1 cup grated cheddar cheese
1 teaspoon salt	1/2 teaspoon garlic powder
2 tablespoons dry milk powder	2 teaspoons yeast

1 1/2-POUND LOAF

1 cup + 2 tablespoons water	3 tablespoons seeded and
3 cups bread flour	chopped jalapeño chile
1 1/2 tablespoons sugar	1 1/2 cups grated cheddar cheese
1 teaspoon salt	3/4 teaspoon garlic powder
3 tablespoons dry milk powder	2 1/2 teaspoons yeast

Double Corn Chile Bread

A Southwestern loaf, filled with some of the favorite flavors of the area.

1-POUND LOAF

2/3 cup water
1 tablespoon margarine
2 cups bread flour
1 tablespoon sugar
1 teaspoon salt

1/2 cup frozen corn kernels,
   thawed and drained
1/4 cup cornmeal
2 tablespoons chopped
   jalapeño chiles*
1 1/2 teaspoons yeast

1 1/2-POUND LOAF

1 cup water
1 1/2 tablespoons margarine
3 cups bread flour
1 1/2 tablespoons sugar
1 1/2 teaspoons salt

3/4 cup frozen corn kernels,
   thawed and drained
1/3 cup cornmeal
3 tablespoons chopped
   jalapeño chiles*
2 teaspoons yeast

*You may substitute canned or fresh green chiles.

Spicy Cornmeal Bread

Use your favorite hot sauce to flavor and heat up this bread. Feel free to change the amount of hot sauce according to your taste, but be sure to adjust the liquid accordingly.

1-POUND LOAF

$^1/_2$ cup water
4 tablespoons hot sauce
1 large egg
2 cups bread flour

1 tablespoon sugar
1 teaspoon salt
$^3/_4$ cup corn meal
1$^1/_2$ teaspoons yeast

1$^1/_2$-POUND LOAF

$^3/_4$ cup water
6 tablespoons hot sauce
1 large egg
3 cups bread flour

1$^1/_2$ tablespoons sugar
1$^1/_2$ teaspoons salt
1 cup corn meal
2 teaspoons yeast

Red Chile Bread

A great red color and strong chile and tomato flavor make this one of my favorites. The sun-dried tomatoes used in this recipe are the dry packaged ones, not the ones preserved in oil.

1-POUND LOAF

1 large egg + water to make
   2/3 cup liquid
1 tablespoon margarine
2 cups bread flour
1 tablespoon sugar
1 teaspoon salt
2 tablespoons dry milk powder

1 tablespoon or less mild red
   chile powder,* to taste
1 tablespoon snipped sun-dried
   tomatoes**
1/4 teaspoon cumin powder
1 1/2 teaspoons yeast

1 1/2-POUND LOAF

1 large egg + water to
   make 1 cup
1 1/2 tablespoons margarine
3 cups bread flour
1 1/2 tablespoons sugar
1 1/2 teaspoons salt
3 tablespoons dry milk powder

1 1/2 tablespoons or less mild red
   chile powder,* to taste
1 1/2 tablespoons sun dried
   tomatoes, chopped**
1/2 teaspoon cumin powder
2 teaspoons yeast

*Use a 100 percent pure chile powder. Supermarket varieties can be as much as 35 percent salt and other additives.

**Sun-dried tomatoes can be difficult to chop with a knife. Just snip them into strips with a scissors.

Chile Cheese Bacon Bread

A winning combination for lovers of Southwestern food. Makes a monumental toasted cheese sandwich. Be sure to watch this one for the first five minutes because the moisture in the green chile is an unknown.

1-POUND LOAF

1/3 cup water
1 teaspoon canola oil
2 cups bread flour
1 tablespoon sugar
1 teaspoon salt
1/2 cup canned green chiles,
    chopped and drained

1/2 cup grated Monterey Jack
    cheese
4 slices bacon,* cooked crisp
1 1/2 teaspoons yeast

1 1/2-POUND LOAF

1/2 cup water
1 1/2 teaspoons canola oil
3 cups bread flour
1 1/2 tablespoons sugar
1 1/2 teaspoons salt
3/4 cup canned green chiles,
    chopped and drained

3/4 cup grated Monterey Jack
    cheese
6 slices bacon,* cooked crisp
2 teaspoons yeast

*No need to crumble up the bacon. Simply break each slice into a couple of pieces and add to the pan. The machine will do the work.

Beer and Cheese Bread

Beer and cheese go well together, and in this recipe they combine to make an excellent bread. Make sure that the beer is flat and at room temperature; I generally measure it out the night before and leave it out until I make the bread.

1-POUND LOAF

1 cup flat beer
2¹/₂ cups bread flour
1 tablespoon sugar
1 teaspoon salt

4 teaspoons dry milk powder
1 cup shredded cheddar cheese
3 tablespoons vital gluten
1¹/₂ teaspoons yeast

1¹/₂-POUND LOAF

1¹/₃ cups flat beer
3¹/₄ cups bread flour
1¹/₂ tablespoons sugar
1¹/₂ teaspoons salt
6 teaspoons dry milk powder

1¹/₂ cups shredded cheddar
  cheese
4 tablespoons vital gluten
2 teaspoons yeast

Cottage Cheese Bread

A high-rising, fine-textured, tasty loaf of bread. This bread rises so high that I'd suggest trying the 1-Pound Loaf first. You may find that it fills up your bread pan.

1-POUND LOAF

2 tablespoons water
³/₄ cup cottage cheese
1 large egg
1 tablespoon margarine

2 cups bread flour
1 tablespoon sugar
1 teaspoon salt
1¹/₂ teaspoons yeast

1¹/₂-POUND LOAF

3 tablespoons water
1¹/₄ cups cottage cheese
1 large egg
1¹/₂ tablespoons margarine

3 cups bread flour
1¹/₂ tablespoons sugar
1¹/₂ teaspoons salt
2 teaspoons yeast

Two-Cheese, Two-Seed Bread

This hearty bread is full of flavor, almost like a three-course meal!

1-POUND LOAF

2/3 cup water
2 cups bread flour
3/4 tablespoon sugar
1 teaspoon salt
2 tablespoons dry milk powder
2/3 cup grated cheddar cheese

2 tablespoons grated Parmesan
   cheese
1 teaspoon sesame seeds
1 teaspoon poppy seeds
1 1/2 teaspoons yeast

1 1/2-POUND LOAF

1 cup water
3 cups bread flour
1 tablespoon sugar
1 teaspoon salt
3 tablespoons dry milk powder
1 cup grated cheddar cheese

3 tablespoons grated Parmesan
   cheese
1 1/2 teaspoons sesame seeds
1 1/2 teaspoons poppy seeds
2 teaspoons yeast

Cheese and Pepperoni Bread

A great tasting, light bread with body. Perfect with eggs in the morning.

1-POUND LOAF

2/3 cup water
1 tablespoon olive oil
2 cups bread flour
1 tablespoon sugar
1 teaspoon salt
2 tablespoons dry milk
  powder
1/3 cup (1 1/2 ounces) provolone cheese, chopped
  or grated

1 tablespoon grated
  Parmesan cheese
1/2 teaspoon garlic powder
1/2 teaspoon onion powder
1 1/2 teaspoons yeast

Add at Beep:
1/2 cup (about 2 ounces) sliced
  pepperoni, slices halved into
  semicircles
1 tablespoon bread flour

1 1/2-POUND LOAF

1 cup water
1 1/2 tablespoons olive oil
3 cups bread flour
1 1/2 tablespoons sugar
1 1/2 teaspoons salt
3 tablespoons dry milk
  powder
1/2 cup (2 ounces) provolone
  cheese, chopped or grated

1 1/2 tablespoons grated
  Parmesan cheese
3/4 teaspoon garlic powder
3/4 teaspoon onion powder
2 teaspoons yeast

Add at Beep:
3/4 cup (3 ounces) sliced pepperoni, slices halved into semicircles
1 1/2 tablespoons bread flour

Pepperoni and Cheese Pizza Bread

Great tasting bread, mouth-filling flavors, almost as good as its namesake.

1-POUND LOAF

2/3 cup water
2 cups bread flour
1 tablespoon sugar
1 teaspoon salt
1/3 cup chopped or grated
   mozzarella cheese
1/2 teaspoon garlic powder
3/4 teaspoon oregano
1 1/2 teaspoons yeast

Add at Beep:
1/2 cup (2 ounces) sliced pepperoni, slices halved into semicircles
1 tablespoon bread flour

1 1/2-POUND LOAF

1 cup water
3 cups bread flour
1 1/2 tablespoons sugar
1 1/2 teaspoons salt
1/2 cup chopped or grated
   mozzarella cheese
3/4 teaspoon garlic powder
1 teaspoon oregano
2 teaspoons yeast

Add at Beep:
3/4 cup (3 ounces) sliced pepperoni, slices halved into semicircles
1 1/2 tablespoons bread flour

Mediterranean Bread

Like many of the breads from the area, this excellent loaf is made without added sugar. Sometimes the simplest are among the best. Use the French or European bread setting.

1-POUND LOAF

2/3 cup water
2 tablespoons olive oil
2 cups bread flour

3/4 teaspoon salt
1 1/2 teaspoons yeast

1 1/2-POUND LOAF

1 cup water
3 tablespoons olive oil
3 cups bread flour

1 teaspoon salt
2 teaspoons yeast

Greek Bread

A taste of the Mediterranean, with the accent on Greece.

1-POUND LOAF

3/4 cup water
1 tablespoon olive oil
2 1/4 cups bread flour
1 teaspoon sugar
1/4 teaspoon salt

4 teaspoons dry milk powder
3 ounces feta cheese, crumbled
10 ripe or Greek olives, pitted
    and quartered
1 1/2 teaspoons yeast

1 1/2-POUND LOAF

1 cup water
1 1/2 tablespoons olive oil
3 cups bread flour
1 1/2 teaspoons sugar
1/2 teaspoon salt

2 tablespoons dry milk powder
4 ounces feta cheese, crumbled
15 ripe or Greek olives, pitted
    and quartered
2 teaspoons yeast

Sesame Seed Bread

This flavorful bread has its origins in the Middle East.

1-POUND LOAF

2/3 cup water
2 tablespoons canola oil
2 cups bread flour
2 teaspoons sugar

3/4 teaspoon salt
2 teaspoons sesame seeds
1 1/2 teaspoons yeast

1 1/2-POUND LOAF

3/4 cup water
3 tablespoons canola oil
3 cups bread flour
1 tablespoon sugar

1 teaspoon salt
3 teaspoons sesame seeds
2 teaspoons yeast

Sesame Seed Oatmeal Bread

The seeds and oats give this bread body and an interesting texture, as well as a Middle Eastern flavoring.

1-POUND LOAF

1 cup water
1 1/2 tablespoons margarine
2 cups bread flour
1/2 cup whole wheat flour
4 teaspoons packed brown sugar

1 teaspoon salt
1/2 cup oats
1/4 cup sesame seeds
1 1/2 teaspoons yeast

1 1/2-POUND LOAF

1 1/2 cups water
2 tablespoons margarine
3 cups bread flour
3/4 cup whole wheat flour
2 tablespoons packed brown
  sugar

1 1/2 teaspoons salt
3/4 cup oats
1/4 cup + 2 tablespoons sesame
  seeds
2 teaspoons yeast

CHAPTER 11

Fruit, Seed, and Sweet Loaves

Many of the breads in this chapter can do double or even triple duty. They can be served with meals or as sandwiches, they can be eaten alone as a snack, or they can be served as a dessert or holiday treat. Regardless, they all tend to disappear fast.

Apple Granola Bread

1-POUND LOAF

1/2 cup water
1/2 cup applesauce
2 tablespoons margarine
1 1/2 cups bread flour
3/4 cup whole wheat flour
1 tablespoon packed brown
   sugar

3 tablespoons dry milk powder
1/2 cup granola
3/4 teaspoon cinnamon
1 1/2 teaspoons yeast

1 1/2-POUND LOAF

3/4 cup water
3/4 cup applesauce
3 tablespoons margarine
2 1/2 cups bread flour
1 cup whole wheat flour
1 1/2 tablespoons packed
   brown sugar

1/4 cup dry milk powder
3/4 cup granola
1 teaspoon cinnamon
2 teaspoons yeast

Apple Almond Raisin Bread

Not a real tall loaf, but big in flavor. A couple of slices at breakfast will set you up for at least a half a day. Be sure to select a bread setting that has a fruit-and-nut audible alert.

1-POUND LOAF

1 tablespoon water
2/3 cup unsweetened apple-
    sauce
2 teaspoons margarine
2 cups bread flour
2 teaspoons packed brown
    sugar

3/4 teaspoon salt
3/4 teaspoon cinnamon
1 1/2 teaspoons yeast

Add at Beep:
1/3 cup raisins
1/3 cup toasted chopped almonds

1 1/2-POUND LOAF

2 tablespoons water
1 cup unsweetened apple-
    sauce
1 tablespoon margarine
3 cups bread flour
1 tablespoon packed brown
    sugar

1 teaspoon salt
1 teaspoon cinnamon
2 teaspoons yeast

Add at Beep:
1/2 cup raisins
1/2 cup toasted chopped almonds

Recipes Using Bananas

In all recipes calling for bananas, I have specified a number of bananas rather than a measured quantity. Why? Because mashing bananas and measuring the mash is messy and a nuisance. Especially since bread machines will turn a ripe banana into liquid in no time at all. I generally just cut the bananas into a few sections and throw them in with the liquid. Let the machine do the work!

The downside to this procedure is that bananas differ in size, so you're going to have to keep an eye on the dough and repair if necessary. I recommend that you do that anyway, so maybe there really is no downside. Give the machine a few minutes to pulverize the bananas. Your dough will look real dry at the beginning but, ironically, most of the time you'll find that the dough is too wet and you'll need to add extra flour. Regardless, just get the dough to that soft and shiny stage, and let it go.

Banana Nut Bread

A tall, light loaf with the flavor of bananas and nuts, plus a crunchy texture.

1-POUND LOAF

1/3 cup water
1 medium ripe banana
1 tablespoon margarine
2 1/4 cups bread flour
1 1/2 tablespoons packed
   brown sugar

1 teaspoon salt
2 tablespoons dry milk
1/3 cup chopped nuts*
1 1/2 teaspoons yeast

1 1/2-POUND LOAF

1/2 cup water
2 medium ripe bananas
4 teaspoons margarine
3 1/2 cups bread flour
2 tablespoons packed brown
   sugar

1 teaspoon salt
3 tablespoons dry milk
1/2 cup chopped nuts*
2 teaspoons yeast

*Pick your favorite nut, or use whatever's on hand. I use walnuts. If the nuts are salted, cut the salt in the recipe in half. If you add nuts at the beep, they'll be larger pieces in the finished loaf. I get lazy at times and throw in large chunks, rather than chopped. That way the machine does the chopping, and there are still pieces of nut in the loaf.

Strawberry Banana Bread

Sweet and flavorful, this bread makes great French toast.

1-POUND LOAF

1/3 cup water	2 1/2 cups bread flour
1/2 cup mashed strawberries	2 teaspoons sugar
1 medium ripe banana	1 teaspoon salt
2 tablespoons margarine	1 1/2 teaspoons yeast

1 1/2-POUND LOAF

1/2 cup water	3 1/3 cups bread flour
3/4 cup mashed strawberries	1 tablespoon sugar
1 1/2 medium ripe bananas	1 1/2 teaspoons salt
3 tablespoons margarine	2 teaspoons yeast

Oatmeal Banana Bread

Good flavor, interesting texture, and a surprisingly good sandwich bread.

1-POUND LOAF

1/3 cup water	2 1/4 cups bread flour
1 1/2 medium ripe bananas	3/4 teaspoon salt
1 1/2 tablespoons canola oil	1/2 cup rolled oats*
1 tablespoon honey	1 1/2 teaspoons yeast

1 1/2-POUND LOAF

1/2 cup water	3 1/4 cups bread flour
2 medium ripe bananas	1 teaspoon salt
2 tablespoons canola oil	3/4 cup rolled oats*
1 tablespoon honey	2 teaspoons yeast

* For best results, use traditional rolled oats rather than quick-cooking oats.

Orange Banana Bread

This moist loaf has a strong orange flavor with a background of banana. Very tasty.

1-POUND LOAF

1/3 cup freshly squeezed
   orange juice
1 1/2 medium ripe bananas
1 tablespoon margarine
2 1/4 cups bread flour
1 teaspoon sugar

1/2 teaspoon salt
1 1/2 tablespoons dry
   milk powder
1 tablespoon orange zest
1 1/2 teaspoons yeast

1 1/2-POUND LOAF

1/2 cup freshly squeezed
   orange juice
2 medium ripe bananas
1 tablespoon margarine
3 1/2 cups bread flour

2 teaspoons sugar
1/2 teaspoon salt
2 tablespoons dry milk powder
1 1/2 tablespoons orange zest
2 teaspoons yeast

Citrus Bread

A tasty bread with a strong citrus flavor. While the recipe calls for zest from three citrus fruits, you can use whatever you have. Just be sure to add the total amount of zest called for in the recipe.

1-POUND LOAF

3/4 cup freshly squeezed
   orange juice
1 tablespoon canola oil
2 tablespoons honey
2 cups bread flour
1 teaspoon salt

2 tablespoons dry milk powder
4 teaspoons orange zest
3 teaspoons lemon zest
2 teaspoons grapefruit zest
1 1/2 teaspoons yeast

1 1/2-POUND LOAF

1 cup + 2 tablespoons freshly
   squeezed orange juice
1 1/2 tablespoons canola oil
3 tablespoons honey
3 cups bread flour
1 1/2 teaspoons salt

3 tablespoons dry milk powder
2 tablespoons orange zest
4 teaspoons lemon zest
1 tablespoon grapefruit zest
2 teaspoons yeast

O.J. Bread

Hey, we're talking orange juice here, not fallen heroes. Regardless, this is a tall, light loaf.

1-Pound Loaf

3/4 cup freshly squeezed
   orange juice
1 tablespoon margarine
2 cups bread flour
2 teaspoons sugar

1 teaspoon salt
2 tablespoons dry milk powder
2 tablespoons orange zest
1 1/2 teaspoons yeast

1 1/2-Pound Loaf

1 cup + 2 tablespoons freshly
   squeezed orange juice
1 1/2 tablespoons margarine
3 cups bread flour
1 tablespoon sugar

1 teaspoon salt
3 tablespoons dry milk powder
3 tablespoons orange zest
2 teaspoons yeast

Orange Marmalade Oat Bread

Oranges and oats are great together in this tall loaf. Use a light crust setting, if available.

1-Pound Loaf

3/4 cup milk
1/3 cup orange marmalade
1 tablespoon margarine
2 1/4 cups bread flour

1 teaspoon salt
1/2 cup rolled oats
1 1/2 teaspoons yeast

1 1/2-Pound Loaf

1 cup + 2 tablespoons milk
1/2 cup orange marmalade
1 1/2 tablespoons margarine
3 1/4 cups bread flour

1 teaspoon salt
3/4 cup rolled oats
2 teaspoons yeast

Orange Anise Bread

Anise gives this light loaf a new flavor twist.

1-POUND LOAF

1/3 cup water
1/2 cup freshly squeezed
    orange juice
1 tablespoon margarine
2 1/4 cups bread flour
1 tablespoon sugar

3/4 teaspoon salt
1 1/2 tablespoons dry
    milk powder
1 1/2 tablespoons orange zest
3/4 teaspoon anise seed
1 1/2 teaspoons yeast

1 1/2-POUND LOAF

1/2 cup water
2/3 cup freshly squeezed
    orange juice
1 tablespoon margarine
3 cups bread flour
1 tablespoon sugar

1 teaspoon salt
2 tablespoons dry milk powder
2 tablespoons orange zest
1 teaspoon anise seed
2 teaspoons yeast

Orange Caraway Bread

Caraway and orange go well together in this tasty loaf.

1-POUND LOAF

3/4 cup water
1 tablespoon margarine
2 cups bread flour
2 tablespoons packed brown
  sugar

1 teaspoon salt
2 teaspoons dried orange peel*
1 teaspoon caraway seeds
1 1/2 teaspoons yeast

1 1/2-POUND LOAF

1 cup + 2 tablespoons water
1 1/2 tablespoons margarine
3 cups bread flour
3 tablespoons packed brown
  sugar

1 1/2 teaspoons salt
3 teaspoons dried orange peel*
1 1/2 teaspoons caraway seeds
2 teaspoons yeast

*Dried orange peel, unsoaked, has the consistency of hardwood. Soak it for at least thirty minutes, and be sure to drain it well before adding.

Cherry Nectar Bread

This short, slightly sweet loaf is loaded with flavor. Use your favorite canned fruit nectar as the liquid, they all work well. Be sure to select a bread setting that has an audible alert.

1-POUND LOAF

7/8 cup fruit nectar
1 teaspoon margarine
2 cups bread flour
1 tablespoon sugar
1/2 teaspoon salt
2 tablespoons dry milk powder

1 teaspoon malt powder
1 1/2 teaspoons yeast

Add at Beep:
1/2 cup dried pitted tart cherries

1 1/2-POUND LOAF

1 1/3 cups fruit nectar
2 teaspoons margarine
3 cups bread flour
1 1/2 tablespoons sugar
3/4 teaspoon salt
3 tablespoons dry milk powder

1 1/2 teaspoons malt powder
2 teaspoons yeast

Add at Beep:
3/4 cup dried pitted tart cherries

Rum Raisin Bread

This delicious bread hardly gets a chance to cool off in my house. If any is left over, it disappears as toast the very next morning!

1-POUND LOAF

2 large eggs + water to make
  ²/₃ cup liquid
1 teaspoon rum extract
1 tablespoon margarine
2 cups bread flour
2 tablespoons packed brown
  sugar

¹/₂ teaspoon salt
¹/₂ teaspoon cinnamon
1¹/₂ teaspoons yeast

Add at Beep:
¹/₂ cup raisins

1¹/₂-POUND LOAF

3 large eggs + water to make
  ³/₄ cup liquid
1¹/₂ teaspoons rum extract
1¹/₂ tablespoons margarine
3 cups bread flour
3 tablespoons packed brown
  sugar

³/₄ teaspoon salt
³/₄ teaspoon cinnamon
2 teaspoons yeast

Add at Beep:
³/₄ cup raisins

Lemon Yogurt Poppy Seed Bread

This tasty bread makes an excellent sandwich loaf.

1-POUND LOAF

1/3 cup water
3/4 cup lemon yogurt
1 1/2 teaspoons margarine
2 cups bread flour
2 teaspoons sugar

3/4 teaspoon salt
1 1/2 teaspoons poppy seeds
2 teaspoons lemon zest
1 1/2 teaspoons yeast

1 1/2-POUND LOAF

1/4 cup water
1 cup lemon yogurt
2 teaspoons margarine
3 cups bread flour
1 tablespoon sugar

1 teaspoon salt
2 teaspoons poppy seeds
1 tablespoon lemon zest
2 teaspoons yeast

Panettone

This Italian sweet bread is one of my favorites. I eat it for breakfast a lot!

1-POUND LOAF

³/₄ cup milk
1 large egg
2 tablespoons margarine
2 cups bread flour
1 teaspoon sugar

³/₄ teaspoon salt
²/₃ cup candied fruit
¹/₂ teaspoon anise seed, crushed
1¹/₂ teaspoons yeast

1¹/₂-POUND LOAF

1 cup + 2 tablespoons milk
1 large egg
3 tablespoons margarine
3 cups bread flour
1¹/₂ teaspoons sugar

1 teaspoon salt
1 cup candied fruit
³/₄ teaspoon anise seed, crushed
2 teaspoons yeast

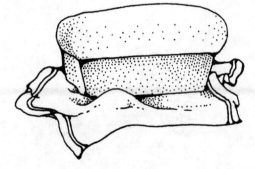

Chocolate Chip Cookie Bread

You'll never guess how this bread got its name. Like its namesake, this bread is delicious with ice cream.

1-POUND LOAF

2/3 cup water
1 tablespoon margarine
2 cups bread flour
2 tablespoons sugar
3/4 teaspoon salt

2 tablespoons dry milk powder
1 teaspoon cocoa*
1/2 cup chocolate chips
1/2 cup walnut pieces
1 1/2 teaspoons yeast

1 1/2-POUND LOAF

1 cup water
1 1/2 tablespoons margarine
3 cups bread flour
3 tablespoons sugar
1 teaspoon salt

3 tablespoons dry milk powder
1 1/2 teaspoons cocoa*
3/4 cup chocolate chips
3/4 cup walnut pieces
2 teaspoons yeast

*Use only unsweetened or baking cocoa. (Sweetened cocoa is used for making drinking cocoa or hot chocolate.)

CHAPTER 12

Spice, Vegetable, and Miscellaneous Loaves

*R*ecipes in this chapter include both the known (onion or garlic bread) and the unknown (peanut butter or malt bread). Also included are some crunchy nut or seed breads.

Dill Bread

This is a nice, light, tall loaf, excellent with fish. If you use the dough cycle, you can then make rolls for great fish sandwiches.

1-POUND LOAF

3/4 cup water
2 tablespoons olive oil
2 cups bread flour
2 tablespoons sugar
1 teaspoon salt

2 tablespoons dry milk powder
3/4 teaspoon dill weed
1/2 teaspoon garlic powder*
1 1/2 teaspoons yeast

1 1/2-POUND LOAF

1 cup + 2 tablespoons water
3 tablespoons olive oil
3 cups bread flour
3 tablespoons sugar
1 1/2 teaspoons salt

3 tablespoons dry milk powder
1 teaspoon dill weed
3/4 teaspoon garlic powder*
2 teaspoons yeast

*You must use garlic powder; garlic salt will not work in this recipe.

Garlic Bread

An excellent garlic-flavored loaf that is perfect with Italian food. Also a tasty sandwich bread, especially with meatloaf or meatballs.

1-POUND LOAF

3/4 cup water
1 tablespoon margarine
2 cups bread flour
1 tablespoon sugar
1 teaspoon salt

2 tablespoons dry milk powder
1 1/2 teaspoons garlic powder*
1 teaspoon onion powder**
2 teaspoons dried parsley
1 1/2 teaspoons yeast

1 1/2-POUND LOAF

1 cup + 2 tablespoons water
1 1/2 tablespoons margarine
3 cups bread flour
1 1/2 tablespoons sugar
1 1/2 teaspoons salt

3 tablespoons dry milk powder
2 teaspoons garlic powder*
1 1/2 teaspoons onion powder**
3 teaspoons dried parsley
2 teaspoons yeast

*You must use garlic powder; garlic salt will not work in this recipe.

**You must use onion powder; onion salt will not work in this recipe.

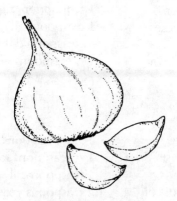

Anise Bread

An unusual bread with a Middle Eastern flavor.

1-POUND LOAF

³/₄ cup water
2 tablespoons margarine
1 cup bread flour
1 cup whole wheat flour
1 tablespoon sugar

1 teaspoon salt
2 tablespoons dry milk powder
1 tablespoon anise seed
2 tablespoons vital gluten
2 teaspoons yeast

1¹/₂-POUND LOAF

1 cup + 2 tablespoons water
3 tablespoons margarine
1¹/₂ cups bread flour
1¹/₂ cups whole wheat flour
1¹/₂ tablespoons sugar

1¹/₂ teaspoons salt
3 tablespoons dry milk powder
1¹/₂ tablespoons anise seed
3 tablespoons vital gluten
2¹/₂ teaspoons yeast

Cottage Cheese Dill Bread

*A fine-textured, good-flavored loaf. Don't be too quick to repair this dough;
it will take a while for the cottage cheese to mix in.*

1-POUND LOAF

2 tablespoons water
³/₄ cup cottage cheese
1 large egg
1 tablespoon canola oil
2 cups bread flour

1 tablespoon sugar
1 teaspoon salt
³/₄ teaspoon dill weed
1¹/₂ teaspoons yeast

1¹/₂-POUND LOAF

3 tablespoons water
1 cup cottage cheese
1 large egg
2 tablespoons canola oil
3 cups bread flour

1¹/₂ tablespoons sugar
1¹/₂ teaspoons salt
1 teaspoon dill weed
2 teaspoons yeast

Mustard Dill Bread

Here's a bread begging for some ham and cheese. Very tasty.

1-POUND LOAF

½ cup + 2 tablespoons water
1 tablespoon Dijon mustard (or
   substitute yellow mustard)
1 tablespoon margarine
2 cups bread flour

1 tablespoon sugar
¾ teaspoon salt
2 tablespoons dry milk powder
¾ teaspoon dill weed
1½ teaspoons yeast

1½-POUND LOAF

1 cup water
1½ tablespoons Dijon
   mustard (or substitute
   yellow mustard)
1½ tablespoons margarine
3 cups bread flour

1½ tablespoons sugar
1 teaspoon salt
3 tablespoons dry milk powder
1 teaspoon dill weed
2 teaspoons yeast

Onion Bread

Onion lovers will think they've gone to heaven; everyone else will just love this excellent loaf.

1-POUND LOAF

$^1/_2$ cup + 1 tablespoon water	1 teaspoon salt
1 tablespoon olive oil	1 tablespoon dry milk powder
2 cups bread flour	$^1/_2$ cup chopped onion
1 tablespoon sugar	1 $^1/_2$ teaspoons yeast

1 $^1/_2$-POUND LOAF

$^3/_4$ cup + 1 tablespoon water	1 $^1/_2$ teaspoons salt
2 tablespoons olive oil	2 tablespoons dry milk powder
3 cups bread flour	$^3/_4$ cup chopped onion
1 $^1/_2$ tablespoons sugar	2 teaspoons yeast

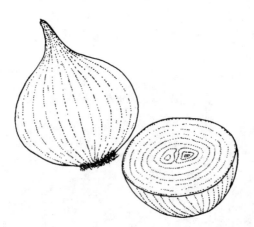

Sun-dried Tomato Rosemary Bread

A couple of personal favorites, sun-dried tomatoes and rosemary, in one great-tasting loaf! The sun-dried tomatoes used in this recipe are the dry packaged ones, not the ones preserved in oil.

1-POUND LOAF

3/4 cup water
1 tablespoon olive oil
1 1/2 cups bread flour
3/4 cup whole wheat flour
2 teaspoons sugar
1 teaspoon salt
2 tablespoons chopped sun-
    dried tomatoes*

2 teaspoons fresh rosemary or
    3/4 teaspoon dried rosemary
1/4 teaspoon garlic powder**
1 1/2 teaspoons yeast

1 1/2-POUND LOAF

1 cup + 2 tablespoons water
1 1/2 tablespoons olive oil
2 1/4 cups bread flour
1 cup whole wheat flour
1 tablespoon sugar
1 1/2 teaspoons salt
3 tablespoons chopped sun-
    dried tomatoes*

3 teaspoons fresh rosemary or
    1 teaspoon dried rosemary
1/2 teaspoon garlic powder**
2 teaspoons yeast

*Sun-dried tomatoes can be difficult to chop with a knife. Just snip them into strips with a scissors.

**You must use garlic powder; garlic salt will not work in this recipe.

Peanut Butter Bread

Kids of all ages love this bread with jam or jelly. Either smooth or chunky style peanut butter will work in this recipe, just pick your favorite. This bread contains a lot of sugar, so select a light crust color, if possible, to prevent a very dark crust.

1-POUND LOAF

1/4 cup water
1/2 cup jelly*
2 cups bread flour
1/4 teaspoon salt

2 tablespoons dry milk powder
1/3 cup peanut butter
1 1/2 teaspoons yeast

1 1/2-POUND LOAF

1/3 cup water
2/3 cup jelly*
3 cups bread flour
1/2 teaspoon salt

3 tablespoons dry milk powder
1/2 cup peanut butter
2 teaspoons yeast

*Use your favorite jelly. If you substitute a jam or preserves, try to measure out more liquid than fruit, or you may throw the liquid-to-flour ratio way off.

Peppermint Granola Bread

Crunchy and chewy with a mint background, this loaf's good with morning coffee or tea.

1-POUND LOAF

³/₄ cup water
1 tablespoon margarine
1³/₄ cups bread flour
¹/₃ cup granola

1¹/₂ teaspoons sugar
³/₄ teaspoon salt
¹/₄ teaspoon peppermint extract
1¹/₂ teaspoons yeast

1¹/₂-POUND LOAF

1 cup water
1¹/₂ tablespoons margarine
2²/₃ cups bread flour
¹/₂ cup granola

2 teaspoons sugar
1 teaspoon salt
¹/₂ teaspoon peppermint extract
2 teaspoons yeast

Oatmeal Bread

An excellent bread for every purpose, a family favorite.

1-POUND LOAF

³/₄ cup water
1¹/₂ tablespoons margarine
1¹/₂ cups bread flour
1¹/₂ tablespoons packed
  brown sugar

1 teaspoon salt
1¹/₂ tablespoons dry milk
  powder
³/₄ cup rolled oats*
1¹/₂ teaspoons yeast

1¹/₂-POUND LOAF

1 cup + 2 tablespoons water
2 tablespoons margarine
2¹/₂ cups bread flour
2 tablespoons packed brown
  sugar

1¹/₂ teaspoons salt
2 tablespoons dry milk powder
1 cup rolled oats*
2 teaspoons yeast

*For best results, use traditional rolled oats rather than quick-cooking oats.

Potato Bread

Using instant potato flakes makes this a quick and easy loaf, without sacrificing flavor.

1-POUND LOAF

1 cup milk
2 tablespoons margarine
2 cups bread flour
2 teaspoons sugar

1 teaspoon salt
2/3 cup instant potato flakes
1 1/2 teaspoons yeast

1 1/2-POUND LOAF

1 1/2 cups milk
3 tablespoons margarine
3 cups bread flour
1 tablespoon sugar

1 1/2 teaspoons salt
1 cup instant potato flakes
2 teaspoons yeast

Anadama Bread

The traditional full-flavored bread, but a bit lighter than most recipes.

1-POUND LOAF

3/4 cup water
2 tablespoons margarine
1 tablespoon molasses
2 cups bread flour

2/3 teaspoon salt
1/3 cup cornmeal
1 1/2 teaspoons yeast

1 1/2-POUND LOAF

1 cup + 2 tablespoons water
3 tablespoons margarine
1 1/2 tablespoons molasses
3 cups bread flour

1 teaspoon salt
1/2 cup cornmeal
2 teaspoons yeast

Malt Bread

Use malted milk powder, available at your grocery store, to make this unusual but tasty bread.

1-POUND LOAF

3/4 cup water
1 tablespoon margarine
2 cups bread flour
1 tablespoon packed brown
  sugar

1 teaspoon salt
3 tablespoons malted milk
  powder
1 1/2 teaspoons yeast

1 1/2-POUND LOAF

1 cup + 2 tablespoons water
1 1/2 tablespoons margarine
3 cups bread flour
1 1/2 tablespoons packed
  brown sugar

1 1/2 teaspoons salt
4 1/2 tablespoons malted milk
  powder
2 teaspoons yeast

Sunflower Nut Bread

A tall, good-looking loaf, with a strong nut flavor.

1-POUND LOAF

2/3 cup water
2 teaspoons margarine
2 1/4 cups bread flour
1 tablespoon sugar
2 tablespoons dry milk
    powder
1 1/2 teaspoons yeast

Add at Beep:
1/4 cup salted sunflower seeds
1/4 cup chopped walnuts

1 1/2-POUND LOAF

1 cup water
1 tablespoon margarine
3 1/4 cups bread flour
4 teaspoons sugar
3 tablespoons dry milk
    powder
2 teaspoons yeast

Add at Beep:
1/3 cup salted sunflower seeds
1/3 cup chopped walnuts

Walnut Bread

A good nutty-flavored loaf that goes well with poultry and some cheeses.

1-POUND LOAF

3/4 cup water
1 teaspoon margarine
2 cups bread flour
1 tablespoon packed brown
  sugar

1 teaspoon salt
2 tablespoons dry milk powder
1/4 cup chopped walnuts
1 1/2 teaspoons yeast

1 1/2-POUND LOAF

1 cup + 2 tablespoons water
2 teaspoons margarine
3 cups bread flour
1 1/2 tablespoons packed
  brown sugar

1 teaspoon salt
3 tablespoons dry milk powder
1/3 cup chopped walnuts
2 teaspoons yeast

PART III

Dough Cycle Recipes

CHAPTER 13

The Dough Cycle

Y ou can use the dough cycle on your bread machine to make a variety of bread variations, from pretzels to pizza. All of these variations require additional steps, including hand shaping and oven baking, but the bulk of the work is done by the trusty bread machine. If you're a newcomer to bread making, don't be intimidated by what appears to be rather complex instructions. Many of the dough cycle creations are really quite simple. And they're worth the extra effort and time for the spectacular results.

Helpful Dough-Handling Tip

After you remove the dough from the machine and punch it down, let it rest for ten to fifteen minutes before you attempt to shape or handle it. This short rest allows the gluten to relax, which makes it much easier to work with. Without a rest, the dough will fight you. It will be a battle to shape the dough, especially to roll it out; and the final shape may be distorted because the gluten will continue to relax after the dough is finally formed. So if the dough is just too springy to handle, if it keeps shrinking or won't hold a shape, just cover it and let it rest for a few minutes and it'll behave.

Baking Breads in the Oven

If you long for bread baked in a regular loaf pan, or find yourself in the mood for rolls rather than a loaf, or want to try your hand at a free-form loaf like a baguette or a boule (a big, round loaf), select the dough cycle and let your machine do all the hard work.

Turn the dough out onto a floured surface, punch down,* and if necessary, knead in enough flour to make it workable. For rolls or a baguette or a boule, shape into the desired shape and place it on a greased baking sheet. For loaves, press or roll the dough into a rectangle and then either roll it up or fold it by thirds into a loaf shape. Press the seams together firmly and place into a greased loaf pan with the seam side down. A one-pound loaf will fill an eight-by-four-inch pan, while a one-and-a-half-pounder will fill a nine-by-five-inch pan. Cover the loaves and set aside to rise in a warm place for twenty to forty minutes, or until doubled.

Crispy Crusts

Black steel pans, or those blackened through use, will produce a crisper and darker crust than pans with shiny finishes. In addition, bread that is oven baked on a baking stone or baking tiles will be crisper than bread baked on an oven rack.

---

* Punching down dough simply means flattening the dough gently to release built up gas. In this case, removing the dough from the bread pan will serve the purpose. If dough is manually mixed and kneaded and then allowed to rise multiple times in a bowl, it is punched down by gently but firmly pressing down on it with the knuckle side of a closed fist, hence the term "punch down."

Bake your bread in a preheated oven, following these guidelines:

Lean breads (little fat or sugar): 375°–425°
Rich breads (considerable fat or sugar): 350°–400°
French breads: 425°–475°

The heat of the oven will spur the yeast into a final frenzy, pushing the dough up one last time. After ten minutes or so, the bread will reach its final shape and start to brown. After this point, it will not affect the bread to open the oven door to check on its progress.

Rolls will bake in ten to fifteen minutes, depending on size, while free-form loaves and loaves in pans have to bake for twenty-five to forty-five minutes. Along with the time guidelines, use your eyes, nose, and ears to tell when it is done. When the bread is golden brown and the smell is starting to make you drool, pull it from the oven and thump it on the bottom with a finger. A dull, solid sound means that it's not quite done, while a hollow sound indicates that it's ready to come out. As soon as the bread's done, cool it on a rack. Let it cool completely before you put it away.

CHAPTER 14

Bagels

*B*agels differ significantly from most breads, but they are relatively easy to make with the help of a bread machine. Keep the following points in mind and you won't go too badly astray. First, while bread dough should be soft, shiny, and pliable, bagel dough should be stiff and belligerent. Second, unlike bread dough, bagel dough is given little chance to rise. We're not after light and airy, we're looking for seriously dense. Finally, because bagels generally contain little fat or sugar, they go stale within a day or two. Eat 'em fast!

Here's how to make bagels:

1. Start by loading all ingredients into the bread pan, select the dough cycle, and press start. Keep a close eye on the dough, adding more flour if necessary to produce a firm, non-sticky ball. Bagel dough should be on the stiff side. Let the machine run through the mix and knead cycles.
2. As soon as the machine has finished the first kneading—that is, before any rise time has started—remove the dough from

the machine. If the dough is sticky or not what you'd call quite firm, knead in flour until it reaches a stiff consistency. If you baby-sat your machine, this shouldn't be necessary. Once the dough is firm, cover it with a towel and let it rest for ten minutes.

3. Divide the dough into 8 pieces. Roll each piece into about a 9- or 10-inch cord. Circle the cord to form the bagel, overlapping the dough ends by an inch. Press together firmly. If the ends don't want to stick, moisten them slightly.

4. Let the bagels rise slightly, for no more than 15 to 20 minutes. Meanwhile, put the required ingredients into four quarts of water and bring it to a boil. When the bagels are ready, carefully slide them a couple at a time into the gently boiling water. A slotted spoon or spatula works well. Cook for 45 seconds on each side, remove, and drain on a dish towel.

5. Place on parchment paper-lined baking pans, brush with lightly beaten egg, sprinkle with toppings, if any, and bake in a 400° oven for 15 minutes. Flip over and bake for another 5 minutes or less, until golden brown.

Water Bagels

These basic bagels, sometimes called New York bagels, are chewy and delicious. This recipe makes eight bagels.

Dough

1 cup water
1 teaspoon canola oil
3 cups bread flour
1 tablespoon sugar

2 teaspoons salt
1 teaspoon malt powder
2 teaspoons yeast

Add to Boiling Water:
1 teaspoon kosher salt
1 tablespoon malt powder

Optional Toppings*
1½ tablespoons coarse
   (kosher) salt
1½ tablespoons sesame seeds
1½ tablespoons poppy seeds

1½ tablespoons caraway seeds
1½ tablespoons chopped garlic

*Use one or more toppings—for best results, don't use more than a total of 1½ tablespoons for eight bagels.

Egg Bagels

Slightly lighter than water bagels, these are perfect for sandwiches. This recipe makes eight bagels.

DOUGH

³/₄ cup water
1 teaspoon canola oil
2 large eggs
3¹/₄ cups bread flour

1¹/₂ tablespoons sugar
2 teaspoons salt
2 teaspoons yeast

Add to Boiling Water:
¹/₂ teaspoon kosher salt
1 tablespoon sugar

Optional Toppings *
1¹/₂ tablespoons sesame seeds
1¹/₂ tablespoons poppy seeds

*Use one or both toppings—for best results, don't use more than a total of 1¹/₂ tablespoons for eight bagels.

Whole Wheat Bagels

Hearty bagels with a natural, earthy flavor. This recipe makes eight bagels.

DOUGH

1 cup water
1 teaspoon canola oil
1 tablespoon molasses
1 1/2 cups bread flour

1 1/2 cups whole wheat flour
1 1/2 teaspoons salt
2 teaspoons yeast

Add to Boiling Water:
1 tablespoon sugar

Optional Toppings*
1 1/2 tablespoons sesame seeds
1 1/2 tablespoons poppy seeds

1 1/2 tablespoons caraway seeds
1 1/2 tablespoons anise seeds

*Use one or more toppings—for best results, don't use more than a total of 1 1/2 tablespoons for eight bagels.

Sourdough Bagels

Adding sourdough to bagels makes them just about perfect. Toast one of these and see if you don't agree. This recipe makes eight bagels.

DOUGH

³/₄ cup water
¹/₂ cup sourdough starter
1 teaspoon canola oil
3 cups bread flour

2 tablespoons sugar
1 teaspoon salt
2 teaspoons yeast

Add to Boiling Water:
1 tablespoon sugar

Topping:
1 large egg, lightly beaten

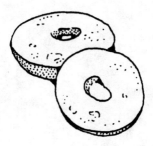

Bagel Variations

If you've been in a bagel shop lately, you know that they offer more flavors than the local ice cream shop. No need to restrict yourself to standard bagels, just take a basic recipe and add your favorite ingredients. Since bagels really don't rise, there is no need to be concerned about "heavy" additions. Use your imagination or pick some additional ingredients from the following list.

apple juice (adjust liquid)
orange juice (adjust liquid)
lemon juice (adjust liquid)
onions (2 tablespoons dried
   flakes, 1 teaspoon powder,
   or 1/3 cup fresh)
garlic (1/2 teaspoon powder
   or 2 medium fresh cloves)
bacon (6 slices cooked crisp)
pepperoni (3/4 cup, about
   3 ounces)

cheese (3/4 cup)
raisins (1/3 cup)
dried cranberries (1/3 cup)
dried cherries (1/3 cup)
dried apples (1/3 cup)
cinnamon (1 teaspoon)
nuts (1/3 cup)

CHAPTER 15

Flatbreads

*F*latbreads are the bread of choice throughout much of the world, especially in warm or hot climates. Use them to scoop up thick soups or stews, stuff them, add ingredients and roll them up, burrito-style. Or just eat them with a meal!

The dough for flatbreads should be on the firm and dry side. It's important to keep an eye on the dough for the first five minutes.

Armenian Thin Bread

Whole wheat flour and sesame seeds are common bread ingredients in this part of the world. This recipe makes six flatbreads.

DOUGH

1 cup water
3 tablespoons margarine
2 cups bread flour
1 cup whole wheat flour
1 tablespoon sugar
1 1/2 teaspoons salt
2 teaspoons yeast

Topping:
1 egg beaten with 1/4 cup water
1/3 cup sesame seeds

1. Load the dough ingredients into bread pan, select the dough setting, and press start. When the machine beeps, remove the dough, punch it down to release gas, and divide into 6 equal pieces. Form into balls, cover, and let rest for 45 minutes.
2. Roll the balls out on a floured surface until they are about 10 inches across; they will be very thin at this point. Transfer them to an ungreased baking sheet, brush with the egg mixture, and sprinkle each one with 2 teaspoons of sesame seeds. Prick the bread with a fork at least a half dozen times.
3. Bake in a 400° oven for 6 to 8 minutes, or until golden brown and slightly puffy. Cool completely before storing.

Middle Eastern Flatbread

You can vary the flavor of this flatbread by substituting anise or fennel seeds for the poppy or sesame seeds. This recipe makes six flatbreads.

DOUGH

1 cup less 1 tablespoon water
2 tablespoons olive oil
3 cups bread flour
1 teaspoon salt
2 teaspoons yeast

Topping:
cold water, as needed
1/3 cup poppy seeds or sesame
  seeds

1. Load the dough ingredients into the bread pan, select the dough setting, and press start. When the machine beeps, remove the dough, punch it down to release gas, and divide into 6 equal pieces. Form into balls, cover, and let rest for 20 minutes.
2. Roll out each piece until thin, about 8 inches across, and place on lightly greased baking sheet. Cover and allow to rise for 15 minutes.
3. Brush with cold water, sprinkle on topping, and bake in a 350° oven for 12 to 16 minutes. Cool completely before storing.

Naan (Indian Flatbread)

Yogurt gives this traditional Indian flatbread a unique and delicious flavor. This recipe makes eight flatbreads.

1/2 cup plain yogurt	2 teaspoons sugar
1/4 cup water	1 teaspoon salt
2 tablespoons margarine	2 teaspoons yeast
3 cups bread flour	

1. Load the dough ingredients into the bread pan, select the dough setting, and press start. When the machine beeps, remove the dough, punch down to release gas, and divide into 8 equal pieces. Form into balls, cover, and let rest for 15 minutes.
2. Roll the balls out on a floured surface until they are 4 to 6 inches across.
3. Place the rounds on a lightly greased baking sheet and bake in a preheated 450° oven for 5 to 7 minutes. Eat warm; cool completely before storing.

Pita Bread

Also known as pocket bread, pita bread is normally cut in half and stuffed with a variety of fillings. This recipe makes eight pieces of pita bread.

1 cup water
3 tablespoons olive oil
2 cups bread flour
1 cup whole wheat flour

1 tablespoon sugar
1 teaspoon salt
2 teaspoons yeast

1. Load the ingredients into the bread pan, select the dough setting, and press start. When the machine beeps, remove the dough, punch down to release gas, and divide into eight equal pieces. Form into balls, cover, and let rest for 15 minutes.
2. Press the balls by hand or rolling pin into 5- or 6-inch rounds. Place on a floured or cornmeal-covered surface, cover, and allow to rise for 30 minutes. Bake in a preheated 500° oven for 8 or 9 minutes. Cool completely before storing.*

*If you're baking these in several batches, allow time between batches for the oven to come back up to the right temperature. It's the very high heat that puffs up the pitas, while a cooler oven will simply produce flatbread. Baking the pitas on a preheated baking stone or pizza tiles will also help.

CHAPTER 16

Soft Pretzels
and Breadsticks

Similar in preparation, soft pretzels and breadsticks are fast and easy to make. However, you must consider your first attempt a learning experience that will be neither fast nor easy. After that it's downhill all the way.

Pretzels

Soft bread pretzels are a delicious snack, with or without a football game, a cold beer, or a jar of mustard. There are several different ways to prepare this recipe, and each will yield a slightly different pretzel.

Soft Pretzels

Make these pretzels according to your own taste. Variation 1 will produce pretzels with a dense, somewhat chewy interior. Variation 2 will yield soft, bread-like interiors. Variation 3 produces a very chewy pretzel with a semisoft interior. Go lightly when sprinkling with the salt, it's easy to overdo it. Whichever variation you choose, you'll get twelve pretzels.

DOUGH

²/₃ cup water   ¹/₂ teaspoon salt
2 cups flour   1¹/₂ teaspoons yeast
2 teaspoons sugar

Topping:
1 large egg beaten with 1 teaspoon water
1 or 2 tablespoons coarse (kosher) salt

1. Load the dough ingredients into the bread pan, select the dough setting. When the machine finishes and beeps, remove the dough to a floured surface. Knead in extra flour, if necessary, to make dough easy to handle. If the dough is fine, punch it down to release gas, cover, and let rest for 10 minutes.

2. Roll out the dough into a rectangle ¹/₂-inch thick. If the dough fights back, let it sit for another 3 or 4 minutes and give it a chance to relax. Divide it into 12 equal strips—a pizza slicer works great. Cover the dough, and form the pretzels one at a time.

3. To form the pretzels, roll or pull each strip into a 15-inch-long rope. Form a circle with the ends overlapped. Then twist the overlapped ends again, and fold back over the bottom of the circle. The finished pretzel should be vaguely heart shaped, with the interior divided into three parts. Sounds complicated, but it's not—trust me.

VARIATION 1: DENSE AND CHEWY

1. Place the pretzels on a greased baking sheet. Brush with the egg mixture and sprinkle with salt.

2. Bake immediately in a preheated 400° oven for 15 to 20 minutes, or until golden brown.

VARIATION 2: SOFT AND BREAD-LIKE

1. Place the pretzels on a greased baking sheet. Mist or brush *lightly* with water, cover, and let rise for 30 to 45 minutes. Brush with the egg mixture and sprinkle with salt.
2. Bake in a preheated 400° oven for 15 to 20 minutes, or until golden brown.

VARIATION 3: CHEWY WITH SEMISOFT INTERIOR

1. Place the pretzels on a greased baking sheet, cover, and let rise for 30 minutes. Bring 2 quarts plus 2 tablespoons of water to a boil. Lower the heat to a gentle boil and gently place a couple of pretzels in the water. Boil for 30 seconds per side, and remove to a paper towel or dish towel to drain briefly.
2. Place the pretzels back on the greased baking sheet, brush with the egg mixture, sprinkle with salt, and bake for 15 to 20 minutes in a preheated 400° oven.

Breadsticks

Whether you eat them as a snack or with a meal, homemade breadsticks are a real treat. Not only can you customize them with your favorite ingredients and toppings, but you can bake them to your exact preference, from soft and light to jaw-challenging extra crispy. Try one of the following recipes, or just use the one-pound version of your favorite bread recipe. (The yield depends on how thick and how long you make the breadsticks. However, a recipe using two cups of flour should make around eighteen six-inch pieces.)

Here are the basic instructions.

1. Start by loading all ingredients into the bread pan, select the dough cycle, and press start. Breadstick dough should be soft but not sticky, since it will be rolled and shaped by hand.

2. Remove the dough to a floured surface at the end of the dough cycle. If the dough is sticky and hard to handle, knead in extra flour until it reaches a workable consistency. Let rest for 10 to 15 minutes.

3. There are two ways to form the breadsticks. The easiest way is simply to roll out the dough into a large rectangle, between ¹/₂-inch and ³/₄-inch thick. Cut into narrow ropes with a pizza cutter. (A little water on the cutting wheel will eliminate any problems with sticky dough.) The ropes can be left as is, or stretched or rolled out by hand if you want them slimmer.

   The other way to form the ropes is to divide the dough into 12 to 15 pieces and roll each one into a thin rope with the palms of your hands. It will take some practice to roll them out evenly.

4. Place the ropes on a greased baking sheet with enough space between for them to grow. Cover, and set aside to rise for 20 to 30 minutes, or until puffy.

5. Brush the breadsticks lightly with cold water and sprinkle with a topping, if desired. Bake in a preheated 400° oven for 15 minutes, or until golden. For an extra-crispy crust, place a shallow pan on the bottom of the oven when it is turned on.* As soon as the breadsticks are placed in the oven to bake, carefully but quickly pour ¹/₂ cup of water into the pan. The water will turn to steam immediately, so get your hand out of the way and shut the oven door at once! Steam burns are some of the most serious and most painful, so learn from reading about it rather than from experiencing it.

The longer the breadsticks are in the oven, the crisper they will become. So experiment a bit to find your favorite consistency. Cool completely after baking, and store in a bread box or paper bag to keep them crisp. If they are stored in plastic, they'll get soft and limp.

---

*Use a heavy-duty pan, like a cast iron skillet, for this job. Lighter-weight pans tend to warp out of shape.

Rosemary Breadsticks

½ cup water
1 tablespoon olive oil
2 cups bread flour
1 teaspoon sugar
½ teaspoon salt

1 tablespoon dry milk powder
2 teaspoons chopped fresh
  rosemary
1½ teaspoons yeast

Parmesan Pepper Breadsticks

½ cup water
1 tablespoon olive oil
2 cups bread flour
1½ teaspoons sugar
½ teaspoon salt

½ cup freshly grated Parmesan
  cheese
½ teaspoon freshly ground
  black pepper
1½ teaspoons yeast

Jalapeño Cheese Breadsticks

½ cup water
1 tablespoon olive oil
2 cups bread flour
1 teaspoon sugar
½ teaspoon salt

⅓ cup grated cheddar cheese
2 jalapeño chiles, stems and
  seeds removed, chopped
1½ teaspoons yeast

Anise Breadsticks

½ cup water
2 tablespoons olive oil
1½ cups bread flour
½ cup whole wheat flour
1 tablespoon sugar

½ teaspoon salt
1 tablespoon dry milk powder
2 teaspoons anise seed
1½ teaspoons yeast

CHAPTER 17

Pizza and Focaccia

We have Italy to thank for these great breads. However, pizza has become so popular in the U.S. that it is no longer classified as a foreign food. It's now as American as the hamburger.

Pizza

Yes, you can make pizza and focaccia at home—and you don't have to devote your entire day to the task! This time-saving tip comes from Jennifer Basye Sander, my editor at Prima Publishing. Rather than making pizza dough in the evening, Jennifer makes hers in the morning, before she goes to work. When the dough cycle ends, she places the dough in a greased bowl, rolling the ball around the bowl to evenly coat it, covers it, and sets it in the frig for the day. After work, she merely has to warm up the dough for about an hour and a half, before finishing off her pizza. (After the dough has warmed completely, press into a pan and allow to rise for 20 minutes.) This procedure not only saves time and trouble, but the long, slow rise in the frig makes the crust lighter and gives it a fuller flavor and a very fine texture.

Basic Pizza Dough

This recipe makes enough dough for a single twelve-inch pizza crust. Double it if you'd like, and put half in the frig. Use the refrigerated dough within two or three days for best results.

Pizza dough can also be frozen. Wrap it tightly in plastic wrap and wrap again with freezer paper. Thaw the dough out in the frig for a day, then allow it to come to room temperature before rolling it out.

½ cup water	¾ teaspoon salt
2 tablespoons olive oil	½ teaspoon freshly ground
1 ½ cups flour	black pepper
1 teaspoon sugar	1 teaspoon yeast

Toppings:
Add any of the following to your pizza dough for a little flavor boost:

1 tablespoon grated Parmesan cheese	1 teaspoon basil
	1 teaspoon thyme
1 teaspoon Italian or pizza seasoning	1 or 2 teaspoons dried chile flakes (vary the heat
1 teaspoon oregano	according to your taste)

1. Load the dough ingredients in the bread pan, select the dough setting, and press start. When the machine beeps, remove the dough to a floured surface and punch it down to expel gas. Press the dough into a greased 12-inch pizza pan. Floured fingers help if the dough is a bit sticky.
2. For a thin crust, top immediately with sauce, toppings, and cheese, and bake in a preheated 400° to 425° oven for 15 to 20 minutes, or until the top is evenly browned and the crust is golden.
3. For a thicker crust, cover and let rise in a warm spot for 20 minutes. Then spoon on the sauce, pile on the toppings and cheese, and bake in a preheated 400° to 425° oven for 15 to 20 minutes, or until the top is evenly browned and the crust is golden.

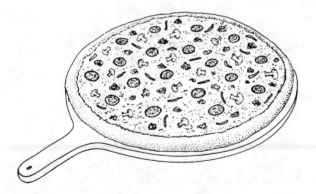

Whole Wheat Pizza Dough

A whole wheat crust is not subservient to the toppings; it competes with and complements them, changing the flavor of pizza into something new but delicious, as always. This recipe makes enough dough for a single twelve-inch pizza crust.

1/2 cup water	3/4 teaspoon salt
2 tablespoons olive oil	1/2 teaspoon freshly ground
1 cup bread flour	black pepper
1 cup whole wheat flour	1 teaspoon yeast
3/4 teaspoon sugar	

1. Load the ingredients into the bread pan, select the dough setting, and press start. When the machine beeps, remove the dough to a floured surface and punch it down to expel gas. Press the dough into a greased 12-inch pizza pan. Floured fingers help if the dough is a bit sticky.

2. Cover and let rise in a warm spot for 20 to 25 minutes. Then top with sauce, toppings, and cheese, and bake in a preheated 400° to 425° oven for 15 to 20 minutes, or until the top is evenly browned.

100 Percent Whole Wheat Pizza Dough

Even heartier! Follow the recipe for Whole Wheat Pizza Dough, but use the following ingredients.

2/3 cup water
2 tablespoons olive oil
2 cups whole wheat flour
1 teaspoon sugar

3/4 teaspoon salt
1/2 teaspoon freshly ground
   black pepper
1 1/2 teaspoons yeast

Sourdough Pizza Dough

I think that sourdough makes nearly everything taste better, and this pizza dough is no exception. One of my all-time-favorite crusts is this recipe with the addition of 1 tablespoon snipped, sun-dried tomatoes and 1 teaspoon of crushed hot chiles.

1/4 cup water
1/2 cup sourdough starter
3 tablespoons olive oil
1 1/2 cups flour
1/2 teaspoon sugar

3/4 teaspoon salt
1/2 teaspoon freshly ground
   black pepper
1 teaspoon yeast

1. Load the ingredients into the bread pan, select the dough set-
    ting, and press start. When the machine beeps, remove the
    dough to a floured surface and punch it down to expel gas.
    Press the dough into a greased 12-inch pizza pan. Floured fin-
    gers help if the dough is a bit sticky.
2. For a thin crust, top immediately with sauce, toppings, and
    cheese, and bake in a preheated 400° to 425° oven for 15 to
    20 minutes, or until the top is evenly browned and the crust is
    golden.
3. For a thicker crust, cover and let rise in a warm spot for 20
    minutes. Then spoon on the sauce, pile on the toppings and
    cheese, and bake in a preheated 400° to 425° oven for 15 to
    20 minutes, or until the top is evenly browned and the crust is
    golden.

Focaccia

Focaccia, a thick Italian flatbread made with various flavoring ingredients, has become popular in recent years simply because it's such good bread. Served as an appetizer with wine or beer, it beats the pants off silly little seaweed and fish-part tidbits! It's easy to make, and it's unbeatable when eaten warm from the oven—and it's not bad the next day, either! The following recipes each make twelve servings.

Olive Focaccia

DOUGH

3/4 cup water
3 tablespoons olive oil
3 cups bread flour
1 teaspoon sugar
1 1/2 teaspoons salt

1 teaspoon freshly ground black
  pepper
2 teaspoons yeast

Add at Beep*:
15 Greek black olives, pitted
  and coarsely chopped

Topping:
4 tablespoons olive oil
6 Greek black olives, pitted
  and quartered

2 tablespoons coarse
  (kosher) salt

1. Load the dough ingredients into the bread pan, select the dough setting, and press start. At the beep, add the olives. When the cycle ends, pull the dough out, punch it down, and knead briefly on a floured surface to release gas. Allow to rest for 15 minutes.
2. Roll or press out the dough into a rectangle to fit a 15 1/2 by 10 1/2-inch jelly roll pan or large baking sheet. Generously grease the pan with olive oil and place the dough in the pan. Drip the topping oil over the top, prick the dough with a fork 20 or 25 times, cover with plastic wrap, and set aside to rise for 30 to 45 minutes, or until doubled.
3. Remove the plastic, press the olive pieces into dough, sprinkle with coarse salt, and bake in a preheated 375° oven for 20 minutes, or until golden brown. Cut into squares and serve warm.

*If your machine doesn't have an "add ingredients" beep during the dough cycle, set a timer and add the ingredients fifteen minutes after the machine starts working

Garlic Focaccia

DOUGH

1 cup water
3 cups bread flour
1 teaspoon sugar
½ teaspoon salt

1 teaspoon freshly ground black
    pepper
2 teaspoons yeast

Dough Additions:
3 tablespoons olive oil
6 garlic cloves, peeled and coarsely chopped

Topping:
6 tablespoons olive oil
2 tablespoons coarse
    (kosher) salt

2 tablespoons freshly grated
    black pepper

1. Sauté the garlic in the oil over medium heat until the garlic is lightly browned, and allow it to cool completely. Load the garlic and the remaining dough ingredients into the bread pan, select the dough setting, and press start. When the cycle ends, pull the dough out, punch it down, and knead it briefly on a floured surface to release gas. Allow to rest for 15 minutes.

2. Roll or press out the dough into a rectangle to fit a 15½ by 10½-inch jelly roll pan or large baking sheet. Generously grease the pan with olive oil and place the dough in the pan. Drip 3 tablespoons of the topping oil over the top, prick the dough with a fork 25 or 30 times, cover with plastic wrap, and set aside to rise for 30 to 45 minutes, or until doubled.

3. Bake in a preheated 375° oven for 20 minutes, or until golden brown. Before serving, drizzle the remaining 3 tablespoons of oil over the bread, season with salt and pepper, cut into squares, and serve warm.

Rosemary Focaccia

DOUGH

1 cup water
3 cups bread flour
1 teaspoon sugar
1/2 teaspoon salt

1 teaspoon freshly ground black
 pepper
2 teaspoons yeast

Dough Additions:
3 tablespoons fresh rosemary
 leaves

3 tablespoons olive oil

Topping:
3 tablespoons olive oil

2 tablespoons coarse (kosher) salt

For Dipping:
4 tablespoons olive oil
1 to 2 tablespoons freshly ground black pepper

1. Heat the oil over medium heat until warm but not burning hot, remove from heat, and add the rosemary leaves. Allow to cool completely. Load the rosemary and oil and remaining dough ingredients into the bread pan, select the dough setting, and press start. When the cycle ends, pull the dough out, punch it down, and knead it briefly on a floured surface to release gas. Allow to rest for 15 minutes.
2. Roll or press out the dough into a rectangle to fit a 15½ by 10½-inch jelly roll pan or large baking sheet. Generously grease the pan with olive oil and place the dough in the pan. Drip the topping oil over the top, sprinkle on the salt, prick the dough with a fork 20 or 25 times, cover with plastic wrap, and set aside to rise for 30 to 45 minutes, or until doubled.
3. Bake in a preheated 375° oven for 20 minutes, or until golden brown. Cut into squares and serve along with shallow saucers filled with the black pepper and dipping oil.

Sun-dried Tomatoes and Onion Focaccia

The sun-dried tomatoes used in this recipe are the dry packaged ones, not the ones preserved in oil.

DOUGH

1 cup water
2 tablespoons olive oil
3 cups bread flour
1 teaspoon sugar
1/2 teaspoon salt
1 teaspoon freshly ground
    black pepper

1/4 cup sun-dried tomatoes,*
    snipped
2 teaspoons yeast

*Add at Beep***
1 cup chopped onion
2 tablespoons olive oil

Topping:
3 tablespoons olive oil
2 tablespoons coarse (kosher) salt
1 tablespoon freshly ground black pepper

1. Sauté the onions in the oil until soft, and set aside to reach room temperature. Load the dough ingredients into the bread pan, select the dough setting, and press start. At the beep, add the onions. When the cycle ends, pull the dough out, punch it down, and knead it briefly on a floured surface to release gas. Allow to rest for 15 minutes.
2. Roll or press out the dough into a rectangle to fit a 15 1/2 by 10 1/2-inch jelly roll pan or large baking sheet. Generously grease the pan with olive oil and place the dough in the pan. Drip the topping oil over the top, sprinkle on the salt and pepper, prick the dough with a fork 20 or 25 times, cover with plastic wrap, and set aside to rise for 30 to 45 minutes, or until doubled.
3. Bake in a preheated 375° oven for 20 minutes, or until golden brown. Cut into squares and serve warm.

*Sun-dried tomatoes can be difficult to chop with a knife. Just snip them into strips with a scissors.

**If your machine doesn't have an "add ingredients" beep during the dough cycle, set a timer and add ingredients fifteen minutes after the machine starts working.

CHAPTER 18

Breakfast Breads

*H*ere are the breads that are so good, it's surprising they're still legal. These are hardly diet food, so I justify eating these by "splurging" only once or twice a year.

Cinnamon Rolls

Who can resist these rolls? And can anyone stop after eating just one? Since the machine does much of the work, there really is no excuse for not making these delicious breakfast treats. The end does justify the means!

Dough

2/3 cup milk
1 large egg
2 tablespoons margarine
2 cups bread flour

2 tablespoons packed brown
   sugar
1/2 teaspoon salt
1 1/2 teaspoons yeast

Filling:
1/3 cup sugar
1 tablespoon cinnamon

2 tablespoons softened
   margarine

Glaze:
1 cup powdered sugar
1/2 teaspoon vanilla

1 tablespoon milk to start,
   more as needed

1. Load the dough ingredients into the bread pan, select the dough setting, and press start. When the machine beeps, remove the dough and punch it down to release gas. Cover and let rest for 10 minutes.
2. Mix the filling ingredients together and set aside. Grease a 9 by 9 by 9-inch pan.

3. Roll out dough into a 9-inch square on floured surface. Spread with 2 tablespoons of softened margarine, and sprinkle all of the filling over the dough. Roll up the dough tightly, dampen the edge, and pinch into roll to seal. Cut into 1-inch slices with dental floss* or a sharp knife, and place into pan, allowing rising room between rolls. Cover and set aside to rise for 1 hour, or until doubled.
4. Bake in a preheated 375° oven for 25 minutes, or until golden brown. Cool them on a wire rack.
5. Mix up the glaze, adding more milk, if needed, until smooth and just thin enough to pour. Drizzle over the rolls while still warm.

---

*A piece of dental floss, looped around the dough roll and pulled together, does an excellent job of slicing off pieces without destroying the roll. Even very sharp knives will tend to flatten out or squash the roll of dough.

Sticky Pecan Rolls

These things are too darn good! The only way I can restrain myself is to just not make them all that often. This recipe makes twelve rolls.

DOUGH

3/4 cup milk
1 large egg
3 cups bread flour

1/4 cup packed brown sugar
3/4 teaspoon salt
2 teaspoons yeast

Filling/Topping:
6 tablespoons margarine,
    melted
3/4 cup packed brown sugar

1 1/2 teaspoons cinnamon
2/3 cup chopped pecans

1. Load the dough ingredients into the bread pan, select the dough setting, and press start.
2. While the machine works, mix together the filling/topping, divide in half, and set aside.
3. When the machine beeps, remove the dough, punch it down, and allow to rest for 10 minutes. Then roll out into a 10 by 15-inch rectangle. Don't worry about exact measurements; close enough is good enough.
4. Spread half the filling evenly on the dough. Roll the dough up tightly, beginning on the long edge. Pinch the edge of the dough into the roll to seal. A little water along that edge can help seal it.

5. Spread the remaining filling/topping on the bottom of a 13 by 9 by 2-inch pan. With a piece of dental floss,* or a very sharp knife, cut the dough roll into 12 equal pieces, and place them in the pan on top of the mixture. Space the pieces evenly—they will rise and fill the whole pan.
6. Cover with a towel and set aside to rise for 30 minutes, or until doubled in size. Bake in a preheated 375° oven for 20 to 25 minutes or until golden brown. Remove the rolls from the oven and immediately turn them upside down onto a large platter. Let the pan sit upside down for a minute before removing it.

*A piece of dental floss, looped around the dough roll and pulled together, does an excellent job of slicing off pieces without destroying the roll. Even very sharp knives will tend to flatten out or squash the roll of dough.

English Muffins

Surprisingly easy to make and even easier to eat, homemade English Muffins are lighter and tastier than supermarket versions. The dough should be a bit on the dry side, so add a tablespoon or so of flour if it looks wet or sticky. This recipe makes twelve to fifteen muffins.

DOUGH

²/₃ cup milk	1 tablespoon sugar
3 tablespoons margarine	1 teaspoon salt
1 large egg	1¹/₂ teaspoons yeast
3 cups bread flour	cornmeal, for dusting

1. Load all of the ingredients except the cornmeal into the bread pan, select the dough setting, and press start. When the machine beeps, remove the dough and punch it down on a cornmeal-covered surface. (If the dough is sticky and hard to handle, knead in a little flour first.)
2. Roll or press out the dough by hand to ¹/₂-inch thick. Flip the dough several times as it is being rolled out, so that both sides are well coated with cornmeal.
3. Cut into circles about 3 inches in diameter, using a cutter or the top of a glass. Cover the muffins and place them in the refrigerator for 45 to 60 minutes.
4. Remove from the frig and cook immediately on a hot, ungreased griddle or cast iron pan set over medium heat. Allow 6 or 7 minutes per side, or until golden brown. They will puff up on the griddle, so space them apart a bit.

Equivalents, Measurements, and Substitutions

Dry Measure

1 1/2 teaspoons = 1/2 tablespoon
3 teaspoons = 1 tablespoon
4 teaspoons = 1 1/3 tablespoons
48 teaspoons = 1 cup
1 tablespoon = 3 teaspoons
2 tablespoons = 1/8 cup
4 tablespoons = 1/4 cup
5 tablespoons + 1 teaspoon = 1/3 cup
8 tablespoons = 1/2 cup
16 tablespoons = 1 cup

Liquid Measure

6 teaspoons = 1 ounce
48 teaspoons = 1 cup
96 teaspoons = 1 pint
dash = 2 to 3 drops
1 tablespoon = 3 teaspoons = 1/2 ounce
2 tablespoons = 1 ounce = 1/8 cup
4 tablespoons = 2 ounces = 1/4 cup
5 1/3 tablespoons = 2.7 ounces = 1/3 cup
6 tablespoons = 3 ounces = 3/8 cup
8 tablespoons = 4 ounces = 1/2 cup
10 tablespoons = 5 ounces = 5/8 cup
10 2/3 tablespoons = 5.4 ounces = 2/3 cup
12 tablespoons = 6 ounces = 3/4 cup
14 tablespoons = 7 ounces = 7/8 cup
16 tablespoons = 8 ounces = 1 cup
32 tablespoons = 16 ounces = 2 cups
1/2 pint = 8 ounces = 1 cup
1 pint = 16 ounces = 2 cups
1 quart = 32 ounces = 4 cups = 2 pints
1 gallon = 128 ounces = 16 cups = 4 quarts

Food Equivalents

Apples: 1 pound = 3–4 medium = 3 cups peeled and sliced
Bananas: 1 pound = 1 1/3 cups mashed
Cheese, American: 1/4 pound = 1 cup shredded
Cheese, cheddar: 1/4 pound = 1 cup shredded
Cheese, cottage: 1 pound = 2 cups
Flour: 1 pound = 3 1/2 cups
Milk, whole: 1 cup = 1/2 cup evaporated + 1/2 cup water
Nuts, shelled: 1/4 cup = 1 cup chopped
Onion: 1 medium = 1/2–3/4 cup chopped
Raisins: 1 pound = 2 3/4 cups
Sugar, white: 1 pound = 2–2 1/4 cups
Sugar, brown: 1 pound = 2 1/4 cups firmly packed

Dry Milk Substitute

Manufacturers' recommendations work best. Here's the rule of thumb:

2 1/2 to 3 tablespoons of dry milk + 1 cup water = 1 cup
    fresh milk

Herbs

Drying concentrates the flavor in herbs, which means that dried herbs are twice as strong as fresh ones. Here's the substitution rule:

If you substitute fresh herbs for dry, use twice as much as the
    recipe calls for.
If you substitute dried herbs for fresh, use half the amount the
    recipe calls for.

Cheese/Water Equivalents

Adding cheese to a recipe also adds moisture, which must be accounted for when adding the liquid ingredients. Here's the general rule:

3 ounces firm, moist cheese (such as cheddar) will add 1 ounce
    (2 tablespoons) of liquid to the recipe.

Mail-Order Sources

Arrowhead Mills
110 S. Lawton
Hereford, TX 79045
(806) 364-0730

Whole grain flours, low-gluten ancient grains

Birkett Mills
P.O. Box 440
Penn Yan, NY 14527
(315) 536-3311

Stone-ground flours

Bob's Red Mill
Natural Foods Inc.
5209 SE International Way
Milwaukie, OR 97222
(503) 654-3215

Natural-food grains and flours plus variety of ingredients

Brewster River Mills
Mill Street
Jeffersonville, VT 05464
(802) 644-2287

Organic flours and meals

Deer Valley Farm
Box 173
Guilford, NY 13780
(607) 764-8556

Grains, seeds, cereals

Ener-G Foods
P.O. Box 84487
Seattle, WA 98124
(800) 331-5222

Organic flours, xanthan gum, egg powder

G. B. Ratto and Co.
821 Washington Street
Oakland, CA 94607
(800) 325-3483

Wide variety of flours and meals

Garden Spot Distributors
438 White Oak Road
New Holland, PA 17557
(800) 829-5100

Whole grains, flours, cereals

Great Valley Mills
687 Mill Road
Telford, PA 18969
(215) 256-6648

Stone-ground flours

Jaffe Bros., Inc.
P.O. Box 636
Valley Center, CA 92082
(619) 749-1133

Organic grains, flours, and meals plus dried fruits, nuts, and seeds

Kenyon Corn Meal Co.
Usquepaugh
West Kingston, RI 02892
(401) 783-4054

Flours and mixes

King Arthur Flour
RR 2, Box 56
Norwich, VT 05055
(800) 827-6836

Basic and unusual flours, along with supplies of every description, including equipment

Maid of Scandinavia
3244 Raleigh Avenue
Minneapolis, MN 55416
(800) 328-6722

Cake-decorating supplies and hardware, plus flavors, extracts, and other ingredients

Mister Spiceman
169-06 Crocheron Avenue
Auburndale, NY 11358
(718) 358-5020

Spices and fruit extracts

Morgan's Mills
RD 2, Box 4602
Union, ME 04862
(207) 785-4900

Stone-ground flour

Mountain Ark Trading Company
P.O. Box 3170
Fayetteville, AR 72701
(800) 643-8909

Organic whole grains, whole grain flours

Niblack Foods, Inc.
900 Jefferson Road, Bldg. 5
Rochester, NY 14623
(800) 724-8883

Barley malt syrup, xanthan gum, gluten flour, flours, bulk yeast

The Vermont Country Store
P.O. Box 3000
Manchester Center, VT 05255
(802) 362-2400

Stone-ground flours and cereals, baking supplies and ingredients

Walnut Acres
Penns Creek, PA 17862
(800) 433-3998

Flours and grains

War Eagle Mill
Rt. 5, Box 411
Rogers, AR 72756
(501) 789-5343

Stone-ground flours and meals

Glossary of Baking and Bread-Making Terms

Baguette   A long, thin loaf of French bread with diagonal slashes.

Batter   A mixture of ingredients and liquid that is thin enough to pour.

Bench proof   The rising stage after yeast dough has been panned, just before baking.

Boulanger   Baker (French).

Boule   A fat, round loaf of French bread.

Bran   The outer layer of a cereal grain, the part highest in fiber.

Brioche   A rich yeast dough traditionally baked in a fluted pan.

Caramelize   The browning of sugar by heating slowly and melting; using heat between 320 and 360 degrees.

Crumb   A term to describe the texture of a baked item, from fine to coarse.

Dough   A mixture of ingredients and liquid stiff enough to be kneaded or shaped by hand.

Durum   A species of hard wheat from which semolina (pasta) flour is milled.

Dust   To sprinkle lightly with flour, sugar, or other substance.

Egg wash   Mixture of eggs and a liquid brushed on baked goods to give them a sheen.

Endosperm   The largest portion of a grain made up of starch and protein.

Farina   Wheat flour or meal (Italian).

Fermentation   The breakdown of carbohydrates into carbon dioxide and alcohol by yeast.

Focaccia   Italian flatbread, often flavored with herbs, always with olive oil.

Germ   The embryo of the cereal grain.

Gluten   A protein that forms into elastic strands when moistened and kneaded; the secret to raised breads.

Kosher salt   Refined salt that does not contain magnesium carbonate.

Leavener   Any ingredient that produces air or gas bubbles, which cause baked goods to raise.

Molasses   Dark colored, sweetish syrup that is a by-product of sugar cane refining.

Oven spring   The rapid and final rise of yeast doughs when heat is applied (generally oven heat), which accelerates yeast growth.

Parchment   Heat-resistant paper used to line baking pans.

Pinch   The amount you can hold between your thumb and forefinger.

Proofing   The second and/or third fermentation stages in making yeast breads.

Punching down   The flattening of yeast dough after rising to expel gas.

Quickbread   Bread made with rapid-acting chemical leaveners (baking powder or soda); also called batter bread.

Scald   Scalding milk is heating it to the point where bubbles appear around the edge of the pan.

Sourdough   Yeast dough leavened with a fermented starter.

Sponge   A mixture of yeast, liquid, and flour that is allowed to ferment and develop a light, spongy consistency.

Sponge dough   A bread dough that has been made from a sponge.

Stone-ground   Flour or meal ground between grindstones.

Straight dough   A bread dough that has been mixed up from the beginning with all ingredients.

Table salt   Refined salt often with iodine added and treated with magnesium carbonate to prevent clumping.

Whole wheat flour   Flour milled from the whole grain including the bran, endosperm, and germ.

Yeast   Microscopic fungus that break down carbohydrates into carbon dioxide gas and alcohol; used in making bread, wine, and beer.

Zest   The thin, colored outer portion of a citrus rind, which contains highly flavored volatile oils.

INDEX